T0165195

If I Can't Be At Your Feet

If I Can't Be At Your Feet

Gunther Denali and Crystal Frakes Brown

A Look at Life with Four Legs and a Tail

iUniverse, Inc.
Bloomington

If I Can't Be At Your Feet
A Look at Life with Four Legs and a Tail

iUniverse books may be ordered through booksellers or by contacting:

iUniverse
1663 Liberty Drive
Bloomington, IN 47403
www.iuniverse.com
1-800-Authors (1-800-288-4677)

Because of the dynamic nature of the Internet, any web addresses or links contained in this book may have changed since publication and may no longer be valid. The views expressed in this work are solely those of the author and do not necessarily reflect the views of the publisher, and the publisher hereby disclaims any responsibility for them.

Any people depicted in stock imagery provided by Thinkstock are models, and such images are being used for illustrative purposes only.
Certain stock imagery © Thinkstock.

ISBN: 978-1-4620-5135-9 (sc)
ISBN: 978-1-4620-5136-6 (ebk)

iUniverse rev. date: 10/25/2011

For Eric, Eddie, Ethan, Baby, Gunther, and Happy,
my everyday sunshine

Contents

A Note from the Author

A *dog* is never treated like "just a dog" in our household. Each four-legged friend has always become a dear member of our family.

Approximately four years ago when I was pregnant with our second son, I frequently had trouble sleeping through the night. As a result, I cleaned, cooked, washed clothes, and did anything else that I didn't get completed earlier in the day secondary to chasing our one-year-old toddler; Gunther never left my side. He continued to be at my feet everywhere I went even in the middle of the night. His never-ending loyalty is a quality that is extremely hard to find, as we all know. At that point in time, I realized I wanted to spread the inspiration of Gunther's wise soul and undying loyalty.

I figured a good way to accomplish this was through pages and pages filled with Gunther's life story; however, I decided the *best* way was to let Gunther tell his own story. *If I Can't Be At Your Feet* is unique in many ways, especially since it is written through Gunther's eyes.

Gunther told me what to put on each page as he cuddled close to me every chance we had time to write; the words literally poured onto the pages. Writing has never been an enjoyable feat for me, that is until I was graced with Gunther as a sidekick and the opportunity to write *If I Can't Be At Your Feet*. Thank you to Gunther Denali and all of our other amazing furry friends who really do make huge differences in our lives. What would we do without you?

Crystal Frakes Brown, August 2011
crystalfrakesbrown@gmail.com
Facebook.com/crystalfrakesbrown

Prologue

To me, life moves as rapidly as a setting sun. Why does life drift away so quickly? One moment, you are a vivacious puppy wrestling with your favorite human; the next moment, you are an old dog needing help to stand.

The moral of life's story: make each moment count.

Happy Fourteenth Birthday, Gunther Denali!

Fourteen Cupcakes and Counting

Even though I have four legs, scratch my butt on the floor, roll in dead animal carcasses, and periodically lick my private parts, my mom and dad treat me like I am one of their direct offspring. Before their sons Eddie and Ethan arrived, Happy and I were their only kiddos. (Happy is one of my daughters who you will get to know later in my tale.)

Mom and Dad used to have so much time for adventuring with Happy and me. However, once our "little brothers" Eddie and Ethan came along, Mom and Dad had much less time for "Gunther follies." They do the best they can, but life just gets busy. We have by no means been denied love, food, or great ear rubs, but we always want more. Speaking of wanting more, let me tell you about wanting more birthdays because of how much fun they are at our house.

"Happy Birthday to Me, Happy Birthday to Me, Happy Birthday Dear Me, Happy Birthday to Me . . . and many more."

Oh, I love, love, love birthdays, especially mine. Today is October 29, 2008, and we are celebrating my fourteenth birthday. What a happy day!

I started my big day by stretching in my king-size bed where I sleep every night. And I mean every night. Well, I have been known to share this bed with my mom and dad from time to time. Although sometimes I have crowded them so much that Mom ended up sleeping on the couch, or I snored so loudly that Dad had many sleepless nights. It is amazing what parents sacrifice for their children, including their four-legged ones.

I rolled over and scratched my back by wiggling back and forth, back and forth, and back and forth while singing a good morning tune. My singing sounds great to me, but I have never had any compliments or an open invitation to sing in church. At least, my singing makes me happy. We should all just focus on what makes us happy and not worry so much about what others think.

I made sure to get a boatload of black hair all over the bed so I would remember where to sleep the next night. Or maybe it was just to tease my parents. Regardless of the reason, I could do anything I wanted because it was my birthday. I finished my morning routine in the bed by shaking my ears tremendously fast and yawning to show off my pearly whites.

Once I was up, I wagged my tail at the birthday decorations strategically hung all through the house. Happy Birthday signs, balloons, orange and black streamers, and colorful party hats decked the halls. The streamers even matched my décor, including black fur and an orange collar. The smell of cupcakes in the oven told me it was going to be an extra special day. Mom always makes white cupcakes with vanilla icing for my special events since chocolate is not good for my digestive system. I couldn't wait to dive into the cupcakes! However, I had business to tend to first so I went outside.

I took my time as usual checking the perimeters to make sure no one had peed in my yard during the night. I strolled along, steadily smelling the air and enjoying the beautiful morning. I said, "Good Morning," to a familiar squirrel by chasing him up a tree. Then I sat in the sunshine and warmed my bones until Dad let me back inside the party house.

I got a Milk-Bone when coming inside as I usually do. Don't tell anyone, but sometimes I pretend like I have to potty when I really don't so I can get additional treats throughout the day. Smart thinking, don't you agree? All doggies need to take note of this sneaky trick.

Once I was relaxing back inside the house, I noticed Eddie, my two-and-a-half-year-old brother, playing with wrapping paper. Yes! I knew there were presents for me somewhere, so I searched the house frantically for them. I always enjoy opening presents and obviously look forward to this on my birthday. Mom and Dad hid my presents from me again today. They were not being mean. They simply have gotten smarter over the years. In the past, anytime I saw presents, I ripped through them immediately like a young child on Christmas morning even if they were not for me. I have opened many other friends' and family members' gifts over the years. For some unknown reason, these curious behaviors never sat well with Mom.

Now Mom and Dad hide presents behind couches, in huge plastic bins, behind closed doors, and in the garage so I will not open them until it is time. I guess I just have to wait until they tell me where they are so I can see what a good boy I have been this year. I hope they have gotten me a mountain of Milk-Bones and my own refrigerator loaded with loaves of cheese bread. Yum! We'll see what the birthday fairy has brought.

For breakfast, Happy and I enjoyed Cheerios and Cheeze-Its in addition to our normal dry dog food. These treats were compliments of Eddie and his wonderful throwing ability from the high chair. Happy and I think Eddie is a godsend with the large quantity and variety of food he shares with us. Ethan is a six-month-old baby and still on breast milk, so he has not started sharing his food with us yet. We definitely look forward to Ethan's days in the high chair, too.

Happy and I also have toys galore thanks to little Eddie and Ethan. Of course as Labrador Retrievers, we love toys of any kind, so we are super happy playing with baby shoes, rattles, and especially Elmo. Chicken Dance Elmo is our favorite.

Next on my birthday agenda was fishing. Fishing is definitely one of my favorite pastimes. Dad took the day off work specifically for my birthday. How lucky am I? I never have to work on my birthday since I don't have a job. I think everyone should have his birthday off from work.

Happy and I suited up to go fishing with Dad on Spring Lake. Spring Lake is the lake we live on year round. It is an all-sports lake that feeds into Lake Michigan: the best of all worlds. Dad and I love fishing together. Happy could take it or leave it, but she went anyway because it was my fourteenth birthday.

It was a beautiful day with sunshine streaming down from the sky. It was a great day to celebrate a birthday, but the shiny rays of sun did not help catch many fish. However, two crappie and two bluegill ended up in the boat eventually, and I wagged my tail like never before. I licked and licked and licked the fish showing my ultimate approval and gave Dad a big smooch on the cheek. I know he loves my kisses, fish breath or not! We kept the fish for a fish fry in which I would definitely be partaking.

After searching for fish, my birthday lunch was ready. Homemade chicken and dumplings with green beans and crescent rolls were waiting for me. We poured this over my usual bowl of food, and I inhaled it instantly. I am very efficient when it comes to gulping down large amounts of food. I wish I could be this efficient at everything I do, such as finding pheasants in the fields.

Next, Happy and I were ordered to sit and stay. We knew it was time for the good stuff. It is always the same schedule every year. The cupcakes were placed on our birthday plates while Dad attempted to put birthday hats on us. Mom snapped pictures throughout this circus routine, and Happy and I drooled all over the floor while waiting patiently for our cupcakes. I know how important it is for Mom to capture priceless moments with her camera, so I tried to be cooperative. However, doesn't she realize I am a dog with a cupcake sitting in front of me? Sometimes I wonder about her.

Once the stage was set, my family sang "Happy Birthday" to me and yelled, "Release!" As you can guess, the cupcakes disappeared into thin air, and Happy and I were begging for more. Don't worry, I did make a wish before I wolfed down my cupcake. Obviously, I can't tell you what I wished for because I want it to come true, but I think you know exactly what my wish was.

Presents followed and a good time was had by all. I tore into all of my gifts as expected, and Happy played with them once they were opened. This is our normal routine. I open the goodies, and Happy takes them away to play with while I continue opening more presents. Naturally, if my birthday surprise is food, I don't hand it over so easily.

Eddie watched in amazement as I ripped into the wrapping paper. My favorite gifts this year were the quacking stuffed ducks and the fourteen pound box of Milk-Bones. Delicious! Dad opened the box and let me dig in for just a few minutes. Thankfully, I did not show anyone my stomach contents later in the day. Mom and Dad were a little concerned about this.

The rest of the day was very festive, including friends coming over to eat pizza and sing "Happy Birthday" to me. It was definitely a party with the works! Deep dish pepperoni pizza is certainly one of my favorite foods. I have been known to seek out leftover pizzas in the fridge without any adult supervision. I can't help it. My nose is just drawn to anything with cheese.

While eating pizza, my birthday buddies rubbed my ears, tickled my tummy, and even brought me some treats. Some of the little bitty friends at my party tried to pull my tail, but I didn't say anything. They didn't know any better. Besides, I thought I could put up with their naughty behavior since they brought me presents. I told you that I love getting presents.

It makes me happy that my parents make a big deal of it when my birthday comes along. I wish all parents did this for their children. It makes me feel extremely loved.

I checked for intruders one more time in the yard before bedtime. I am a little paranoid now about criminals because we watch lots and lots of Crime Scene Investigation shows. You never know who is around the corner, so I must make sure our home is safe and protect my family! My grandpa constantly reminds me of the dangers lurking around all of us, so he helps keep me on my toes. Of course, Grandpa may take it a bit too far because he locks the door when he goes in the backyard so no one "slips up" on him. I guess it is a good idea, in theory, until he locks himself out and is stuck outside with a possible approaching criminal.

Once I was back inside our cozy house, I jumped into our king-size bed and fell asleep first, taking up way more room than I should. As I was soundly sleeping and most likely snoring, I woke up for a few seconds as Dad repositioned me so we could all fit in the bed for the evening. What a fun birthday celebration! I wish every day could be like my fourteenth birthday.

Slip-Sliding Away

Almost eleven months have passed since my fourteenth birthday bash, and now it is September 25, 2009. We are all praying I will make it to my fifteenth birthday. Of course, if I do make it to my fifteenth birthday, I can't party like I used to because I have had a major decline in health over the past few months. I feel like my life is slowly slip-sliding away.

Currently, I have major difficulty standing up by myself and can no longer jump into my king-size bed. I even slide down the steps or fall down them sometimes when trying to go in and out of the house to potty. Often times, I have accidents in the house, leaving a big mess for my parents to clean. Mom even recently yelled, "I don't have time for this!" Even though I knew she was talking about the urine trail I left across the living room carpet, I couldn't help but think she meant she didn't have time for me anymore. My timing wasn't very good either since my accident was right after Eddie pooped in the potty and Mom found Ethan stirring it with a kitchen spatula. I think she actually meant she didn't have time for any of our craziness. Eddie, Ethan, and I sure know how to push Mom's buttons.

Unfortunately, when my accidents happen, I don't have the convenience of going to the closet to get the mop to casually clean it up myself or drive to the store to quietly pick out personal items to prevent a future accident. Instead, I must have accidents on the floor for everyone to see. Many times I have them when no one is home to let me out the very second I have the urge to go to the bathroom. Can you imagine how embarrassing this is for me? I absolutely hate disappointing my family. My bladder is definitely not like it used to be.

Mom and Dad don't want to lift me up in their bed anymore since they are afraid I will have an accident and ruin their mattress. I would buy them ten new mattresses if I could. I am also deaf now in addition to my other declining health conditions. Therefore, if I can't sleep where I can physically touch Mom and Dad at night, I feel they are unprotected, which goes completely against my nature. When I am next to them sleeping, I know they are safe and will never let anything bad happen to them regardless of how old and frail I become.

Luckily, with lots of practice, I have gotten really great at reading lips so I still know what my family is saying throughout the day. Mom also uses hand gestures constantly when speaking; I can tell what she is saying just through watching her hands dance in front of her. Grandpa always says, "Your mom wouldn't be able to talk if you held her hands still." I think he is right.

Once I am asleep on the floor filled with worry, I wake up multiple times during the night with difficulty breathing. My laryngeal paralysis causes this trouble breathing. I learned about this at my veterinarian's office a few years ago. Apparently, this is a common diagnosis among older Labradors. This condition results in weakened throat muscles, making it hard for me to breathe well while playing and exercising. My doctor said that I could have surgery, but he was not sure I would survive the anesthesia at my age. Therefore, Mom and Dad decided to forego this procedure, and I am extremely glad they did.

Unfortunately, I can no longer swim, run, bike (just checking to see if you are paying attention), and play Frisbee due to my sore hips, decreased breathing ability, and massive loss in weight recently. Trust me, my desire to do these things is no different than when I was two years old. My body just won't allow me to do these fun activities anymore. Getting old is definitely not for the weak.

Please take it from me: *play, play, play as hard as you can for as long as you can!* I hope to inspire an honest yet playful and happy life loaded with never-ending, fun-filled adventures because this is the only way to live. I wish this for each and every person in this wide, wide world.

Oh, how rude of me! Please let me introduce myself before I get too keyed up any further about telling you how to live your own life. My name is Gunther Denali Brown. I am a black Labrador Retriever who loves many things in this exciting world and has had countless adventures. Let's just start at the beginning. I'll take you back to a very dear place in my heart: Indiana University in Bloomington, Indiana. Let's go Hoosiers!

Hoosier Pup

On October 29, 1994, I was born into a family of nine puppies. My birth mother was named Godiva Lorne, a chocolate Labrador Retriever, and my birth father was named Sire Adore's Night Spirit, a black Labrador Retriever. I lived with my mom, brothers, and sisters on a quaint little street called Dekist in Bloomington, Indiana, near Indiana University.

Indiana University (I.U.) is such a beautiful and exciting place to play. I used to smell the flowers and roll in the soft green grass in Dunn Meadow when wandering through campus. As I explored, I met many pretty girls. Wow! This should definitely be inspiration to go on to college for you young men out there. Most of the Hoosier beauties were very happy to meet me. They thought I was really cute and loved to pet my soft ears. What an ego boost for me. Of course, the I.U. girls were out of my league, but I will never tell all of my secrets.

Even as a puppy, I had a few late nights exploring campus and Kirkwood Avenue. Kirkwood is loaded with shops, restaurants, and bars for Hoosiers to enjoy. I clearly remember sneaking out for my first night on the town after my mom, brothers, and sisters were fast asleep. I bounced out the front door to see what I could see. I strolled down to Kirkwood Avenue to see for myself what it was like. I did a little window shopping, but I didn't see any clothes with holes for a tail.

Next, I stopped at Nick's English Hut to catch a glimpse of the Hoosiers playing basketball on television through the front door. However, I couldn't see any part of the game because of the long line of people waiting to get in for basketball festivities. No worries. Bloomington is full of fun stuff to do, so I ran over to Upstairs Pub to hang out and learn to play pool. The big guy at the front door kept petting my head and saying, "What a cute puppy." He even had other people come out to play with me. I was glad to meet the new friends and have the unexpected ear rubs, but I really wanted to go inside and relax. I politely asked, "Excuse me, may I come in?" I guess the big guy didn't speak dog, so he only heard, "*Bark. Bark. Super polite bark.*" He just smiled and said, "I gotta go pal," and shut the door. Well, so much for my attempt to play pool at a happening spot.

I didn't meet any other furry friends out that night, but I got to do a lot of people watching, which I enjoyed. Bloomington, also known as "B-Town," welcomes a diverse crowd, so I never felt out of place and saw lots of interesting people. People watching always makes me hungry, just like any other activity, so I bounced up the steps to a Mexican restaurant named LaBamba. LaBamba was so crowded that I figured I could sneak in there easily and no one would notice. Lucky for me, two girls walked out right before I entered the late-night establishment. Apparently, one of the girls was not feeling well. I guess she had the flu, so her other friend gave me a whole burrito and said, "Have fun with this, buddy." How lucky am I? I quickly tore the burrito wrapper off to find steak and chicken inside. It was good to be in the right spot at the right time.

With a very full tummy, I slowly ran home and sneaked inside my house before anyone knew I was missing. Since this virgin journey went well, I took advantage and had many more adventures in "B-Town."

I definitely had some very wild times at I.U. However, I am not going to share all the details with you or my grandkids. Sorry! I just have to keep you guessing.

One day in April of 1995, I decided to go exploring down the street to see who I could meet. I have always been a social butterfly; I was excited to meet new friends anytime the chance presented itself. My first stop was at 210 Dekist Street where I found a guy named Scooter. Apparently, Scooter really wanted to play Frisbee when I bounced into his yard, so I thought I would humor him. Scooter and I ended up having so much fun! We played and played until Eric, a friend of Scooter's, came home after his classes. I guess college kids really do go to class.

Immediately, I clumsily ran to Eric to introduce myself and give him a sniff. He was full of belly and ear rubs and came bearing a leftover piece of pizza. How did he know this was the way straight to my heart? I can't explain how big his smile was when he first saw me. I know I have continued to bring Eric huge smiles over all of our years together. Unfortunately, I have also caused him a few frowns due to my outrageous curiosity. I will explain later.

On the day I met Eric, he said, "You are the cutest roly-poly puppy I have ever laid eyes on; you remind me of a little tank with legs." Eric and Scooter were not sure where I came from, so they started putting up signs to try and find my home. I was having tons of fun, but eventually I realized it was getting late and needed to go home. I started wandering back down to my house, and my new buddies followed me. Godiva's human mom and dad saw the three of us strolling down the street. Eric ended up chatting with them. He discovered I was one of Godiva's puppies and lived only two houses away from him. Godiva's parents explained that I could go home with Eric if he desired to have a pudgy black puppy in his life.

At once, Eric called his parents to ask if there was room for me at their house in Indianapolis since he would soon be leaving Bloomington after graduation. At the time, his mom and dad had two other pooches.

Being the dog lovers that they are, they had no hesitation about adding another four-legged lover to their family. With graduation money from Eric's papa and nana, Eric brought me into his life permanently. Ever since that day, I have been the happiest pup alive. I never dreamed my random stroll down Dekist Street in Bloomington, Indiana, would shape my entire life and lead me to many amazing friendships. This proves that life is a constant expedition and can change as quickly as the shores along Lake Michigan.

Before I met Eric, I knew that my momma Godiva needed help raising me. She didn't have any money and relied on her human mom to provide for us. I didn't see much of my canine dad, Sire Adore's Night Spirit, once I was born, so I knew Momma and I were on our own. However, with a name like Night Spirit I really didn't factor him in as a stable part of my life in the first place. This led me to thinking about career decisions in case I needed to support my momma and siblings.

It was very convenient that we lived near a college campus because the opportunities were limitless for me. I thought about meteorology. The weather has always been very interesting to me. Of course, I would consistently call for sunshine with blue skies because I feel positive thinking will get you very far in this crazy world. Besides, who doesn't love a sunny day with a brilliant blue sky? Official Taste Tester sounded good, but I love to run and play; eating food all day, everyday, might not have been the best thing for my health in the long run. In addition to Official Taste Tester, I thought about being a bouncer at one of the bars on Kirkwood Avenue where lots of the Hoosier action happens. I decided against this because my momma Godiva was not too excited about this possible career choice. Also, I would hate to have to throw Scooter and Eric out periodically when they got too fired up. Certainly, the most logical choice was to be a Privates' Investigator. Obviously, this skill comes naturally to me, but I wasn't sure if I would be able to make a living at this. Sailboat captain was another possible career path I considered. I thought I could sail beautiful women all over the world to their favorite island destinations. However, Bloomington is a landlocked location so I would have to move far away to do this. Again, Momma was a little weary of this idea.

Luckily, I stumbled into Eric's life, and he walked into mine, so I no longer had to find a career. I was certainly dreading trying to find an interview suit with four legs and space for a tail. It was such a nice feeling to know my new dad would take care of me, and I no longer had to burden Godiva. She never ever said that I was a burden, but I did not want her to struggle with caring for all of my siblings and me by herself. It is tough to be a single canine momma. I love her very much for all she has done for me.

When I was born, my momma told me that our time together was limited. Being the curious puppy that I am, I asked, "Why?" Momma said, "Honey, I know you will bring someone else much, much happiness. I can't and won't be selfish and prevent another person from a lifetime of smiles thanks to you." I was very excited about making others happy, but I knew I would miss Momma like crazy. To reassure me, she said, "You will never be without me. A little piece of me will always be with you."

The day eventually came when I had to say goodbye to Godiva. Sadly, we all have to say goodbye to the ones who mean the most to us at some point in our lives. It doesn't matter if it has been six months or sixty years, I think it is never easy to say goodbye. This is why we must make each moment count.

Mom licked my ears and gave me a kiss on the face when Eric came to take me home with him. She said, with tears in her eyes yet a smile on her face, "I love you, baby boy. Make me proud." I was too choked up to say anything, so I gave her a big lick on the cheek and a huge tail wag. Off I went with my new person Eric with watery eyes yet a happy heart.

I immediately became attached to Eric. At that point, I thought of him as my dad and always have ever since. Obviously, as a six-month-old pup, I learned to rely on Eric for everything. From day one, I always wanted to be by his side and make him proud of me. I think it is natural for pets to become acclimated to "their people" since many pets leave their natural mommies and daddies at a very young age.

Even though I absolutely loved every part of being Dad's new puppy, I still missed Momma from time to time. Whenever I got a little bummed, I used to bark until she barked back. This is why doggies bark sometimes even though it appears there is no reason for it. We don't have telephones, email, Facebook accounts, or faxes, so we have to be creative to keep up on the gossip with our families and friends. When there is a lot of distance between dogs, other dogs have to help pass the messages along the way. Thankfully, Momma and I had many friends in between us who were more than willing to pass our communication back and forth.

Dad named me Gunther Denali Brown. Denali is in reference to the native name for Mount McKinley meaning "The Great One." Mount McKinley is located in Alaska's Denali National Park and is the tallest peak in North America. Dad knew from the very beginning that I would be a great friend and a mighty influence in his life as well as the lives of others close to him. Apparently, he was right.

My first summer with Dad was very eventful. No summer school, just us guys spending the summer together working and playing. Well, I guess we can call it work. Dad was on the lake patrol for Sweetwater and Cordry Lakes in southern Indiana, and I was his right-hand man. I enjoyed being on the boat and taking a swim anytime I got the chance. I also got the hot babes in bikinis to look our way often. Obviously, neither one of us minded this one little bit. I entertained the kiddos playing along the shoreline frequently, too.

I interacted with everyone I met whether it was with a friendly tail wag, a lick on the cheek, or a swim to shore. I have to admit that I have developed some remarkable habits over the years. Back in my early swimming days, I had a routine of swimming people to shore even if they did not need the help. For fun, I used to swim up to a kiddo playing in the water, gently grab onto one of his arms with my mouth, and safely tow the child to shore. Yes, this did evoke many anxious looks and a few choice words from parents, but the kids loved every second of their free ride. I know my jaws are so powerful that I could have easily crushed a tiny child's arm, but instead I was always Mr. Gentle.

Dad was not excluded from this interesting swimming pattern of mine. He used to get a little frustrated with me when he was trying to swim for exercise. Each and every time, I paddled over to him, grabbed one of his arms, and swam him back to shore. He didn't get many laps in when I was around. Now, we both wish we could go back to those days again when I could still swim and do it very, very well.

In the fall, Dad started school in Indianapolis, so we moved into his parents' home on the east side of Indianapolis. Unfortunately, I did not see much of my dad at this time due to his extreme schedule as a first-year medical student. Anytime Dad was home, I tried to please him any way I could. I brought a pillow or shoe in my mouth to greet him, followed him everywhere he went, and slept on anything that smelled like him. Anytime Dad was at school, I rested in front of the door so I could be the first one to greet him when he arrived. Obviously, sleeping by the door meant anyone coming into our house had to get through me first, so this was also my way to protect everyone while Dad was away.

Even though he was extremely busy with his new agenda, Dad always made some time for me. Countless nights he came home from studying around midnight, and I waited for him asleep by the door. Dad always felt bad that he had been gone all day long, so he used to hop on his bike and say, "Let's go!" He rode his bike around the block while I chased him carrying a piece of firewood in my mouth. Sometimes we even went across the street to Heather Hills Elementary School's playground and played Frisbee into the wee hours of the night. Then we came back home and sometimes fell asleep on the floor beside each other while Dad was petting me. He was always amazed at my speed and strength in my earlier years while playing, running, and hunting. If only I had a quarter of the energy and strength now that I had as a pup. Well, I may be weaker, but I am definitely wiser. At least, I think I am. I know to this day that Dad still thinks of these late-night excursions together as some of his favorite memories with me. I agree.

Although Dad was a very busy student, he apparently had some extra time because he was hanging out with a new friend he met on campus. I soon found out this new friend was a *girl*. Little did I know that this *girl* would eventually become my human mom.

Dad dated this *girl* named Crystal for a few months before he introduced her to me. He actually let Crystal meet his immediate family first before he let the two of us come across each other. How funny! Dad told me that he wanted to make sure Crystal was worthy before she was allowed to meet me. He knows how attached I get to his friends, so he took extra precautions to protect my sensitive side. Hey, dogs have sensitive sides too, and I am very proud of mine.

Finally, Dad came home to pick me up one night so I could meet Crystal. Dad and Crystal were studying together at his dad's office, so Dad took me back to the office to greet her. I couldn't wait any longer. My curiosity was getting the best of me. I ran through the door as quickly as I could and shot through the office like a lightning bolt looking for her. And there she was: hazel eyes staring happily at me, blonde hair pulled back in a ponytail, large stack of books in front of her, hot cup of coffee in hand, and a huge smile on her face when I came running to her. I knew I had seen a similar smile like this before. It hit me right then and there that I saw this same massive smile on Dad's face when he first met me. I am absolutely no matchmaker. However, I knew from that second on that they would be together forever and that Crystal would become my human mom. Without delay, I gave Dad the paws up sign, and the rest is history.

I was ecstatic that Dad found Crystal because she absolutely loved spending time with me. Crystal was always thrilled to play with my rambunctious yet gentle self. She kept me entertained with frequent walks and runs in downtown Indianapolis. I also stayed with her many nights in her apartment which she really appreciated. I protected Crystal and her roommates and kept Crystal warm many, many nights. I love my job!

I think I made Crystal's college life more fun than it already was. Not only did I take her fun meter to a new level, but I was also a fantastic study buddy. She recited her work to me often, and I never got tired of hearing her talk. Actually, I looked forward to study time with her because she usually pet my black shiny coat for hours as a stress reliever when she was cramming for her exams. I thoroughly enjoyed every minute of this. Luckily, my appetite always stayed on food instead of her homework.

I thank Crystal and Dad for all of the study time they shared with me. It is amazing how much I learned through their college years without paying my own tuition. I know their college days have helped me to share my tale with you today.

Countless times classes got in the way of having fun with Dad and Crystal. At this point in time, I decided I wasn't going to sit around like a bump on a log. Instead, I was determined to entertain myself, which I did with flying colors.

"What should I entertain myself with today?"

Self Entertainer

As **The Self Entertainer**, I learned lots of new tricks. Let's start with my favorite: the refrigerator. I have always liked to eat, so I thought I should figure out my food sources right away. I soon learned the massive metal box in the kitchen held food beyond my dreams. Eventually, I learned these wonderful objects are called refrigerators, and I decided to get very comfortable with their features.

Yes, I taught myself to get in the fridge whenever I wanted whether I was hungry or not. Dad and his parents realized this quickly when they came home frequently to a refrigerator with the door standing wide open, multiple food items missing, and the remaining food at room temperature. At the time, I had a Brittany Spaniel named Molly inside to play and get into trouble with simultaneously. However, Dad knew I always instigated the refrigerator robberies because Molly never did this as the lone inside dog.

I used to pretend that I was in Las Vegas at the Bellagio Buffet when I opened the fridge door. (I have learned about many exciting food destinations from Mom and Dad's travel stories.) I used to eat a variety of food, including pizza, chocolate cake, loaves and loaves of cheese and French bread, whole lasagnas, and pounds of uncooked meat. I was not picky then, and I'm still not picky today regarding what I like to eat.

Obviously, Dad did not realize that my new behavior would transcend to all of the refrigerators that he and Crystal would own for my entire lifetime. It did not matter the style of refrigerator, whether the freezer was on the top or bottom or if it was a side-by-side design. I am proud to admit I have gotten into all of them single-handedly.

The first time Crystal stopped by Dad's parents' house in Indianapolis to visit us, the refrigerator had multiple bar stools in front of it, plus a large bungee cord holding the door shut. The fridge door didn't shut anymore at this point in time because I had eaten the seal off the door to make my grocery robberies more efficient. This led to Dad setting up bar stools and bungee cords to keep the door closed, the food cold, and his curious puppy away.

When Crystal stopped by our house periodically, she thought the fridge situation was very strange, but she decided not to ask questions. Comically, she soon discovered that I simply liked to get into the refrigerator without asking permission. The bungee cord and barstools were one hundred percent Gunther prevention.

While playing refrigerator inspector, I learned I liked just about every food under the sun except raw veggies. Dad can keep his carrots, lettuce, and tomatoes to himself. It looks like I am definitely not a vegetarian.

Did I mention I like trash cans almost as much as refrigerators? I never understood why I got into so much trouble when I dove in and helped myself to the mysterious contents in the trash. The goodies in the trash were obviously going to be thrown away. Why waste them? This was my own way of taking out the trash and helping the environment. Besides, I thought Dad would be proud of me.

Apparently, it is frowned upon when your eighty-eight pound furry friend knocks over the fifty gallon trashcan at the bachelor house and leaves wrappers all over the floor. This happened during Dad's third year of medical school in 1997 when we lived with some of Dad's good friends on Tremont Street on the west side of Indianapolis. Lucky for me, one of Dad's roommates named Chubby had a yellow Labrador named

Kodi for me to pal around with. I got to play with Kodi everyday, and obviously, we got into our fair share of trouble. Kodi is six months older than I am and was also born in Bloomington, Indiana. Maybe the secret to longevity is in the Bloomington water? This is definitely something for us to ponder. During our dads' long hours away, whether at work, school, or The Working Man's Friend (a restaurant/bar down the street from us), we knocked over the trash frequently and pigged out. Chubby is an excellent cook, so the trash was always a delicacy after he whipped up a tasty meal.

Unexpectedly, Crystal and her mom Susie showed up one day immediately after Kodi and I raided the trash. Admittedly, we made a huge mess this particular day. The funny part is that Crystal and Susie let Kodi and me out to potty, gave us Milk-Bones, and left the mess on the floor because they were very short on time. Crystal did not tell Dad about this until years later.

I amused myself in other ways besides food, including taking Dad's mom for walks. Yes, I said that correctly. One specific stroll stands out to me due to what happened during the walk. I am sure you can guess that I have a great affinity for cats since I dream about them and I am a dog. Cats present a great challenge to the canine population with their swiftness and quirky characteristics.

When Dad's mom Anne was taking me on a walk through the neighborhood on a beautiful summer afternoon, a cat ran in front of us. Immediately, I thought, "Game on!" so I took off running at my top speed, pulling and eventually dragging Anne behind me. Anne tried to stop me, but I continued to drag her through the grass after the cat. Of course, I never in a million years meant to hurt her; but I could not let this cat get the best of me. Anne is a very forgiving person; I knew she would understand. Unfortunately, the cat ended up getting away, so I slowed down. Anne stood up and gave me a piece of her mind while she looked down at all of the grass stains on her outfit. Oops! I know not to bite the hand that feeds me, but I couldn't process the situation fast enough when the cat was teasing me.

A few years later, Crystal also took me on a memorable walk during which a cat intervened on our happy amble. As we were walking down Tremont Street, a cat darted out in front of us. I lurched to go after the cat and immediately felt my body stop in mid-air. Crystal yelled, *"Gunther, no! There is a car coming!"* She wrapped one arm around a huge tree branch and held my leash as tight as she could with the other hand to stop me. Right away, I realized that Crystal had kept me from getting hit by a car, and I avoided dragging her across the street to chase the cat. I know Crystal's arms were really tired the next day, but at least this is minor compared to what could have happened that day.

Regrettably, I started entertaining myself with hobbies that fell on the more expensive side than Shout for grass stain removal. I needed to fill my down time one afternoon and decided to investigate a bear rug that hung on the wall in the living room. I felt as if the whole family was in danger with this huge bear just watching us every day and night. I knew I needed to take his claws so he did not try to attack all of us when we had our guard down. Without delay, I jumped on the couch and started to devour his claws. At the time, I thought this was a great time consumer and a healthy snack, but I soon found out that I had made much better decisions in the past.

Anne, a third-grade teacher, arrived home first from school and almost passed out when she saw what I had done. She sent me outside right away. I listened through the window and heard her call Dad at school. She said, "Eric, everyone is fine, but it has not been a good day at home!" I personally thought it was a perfect day, but I would soon find out differently. Dad arrived about twenty minutes later, and he was not happy with me.

I was forced to stay outside most of the evening, and I got absolutely no dinner. Dad said that the claws were plenty of food for me that night. I think Dad's father Ed actually felt sorry for me because Dad was very mad at me. I really do not remember Ed saying much about the whole situation. I am glad I dodged that bullet.

All evening I tried to say, "I was only protecting you because I love you," but for some reason no one heard me. I believe if people focused on listening more than speaking, this world would be a much better place.

Anyhow, I guess all eighty-eight pounds of me caused quite a bit of damage to this brown bear from Kodiak Island in Alaska. To some of you, de-clawing an Alaskan brown bear might not seem like much of a problem. However, to those of you who hunt, you are squirming in your seats right now. Ed had taken a trip to Alaska years prior and shot this bear himself. This was a very expensive and once-in-a-lifetime excursion. The only reason I know this information is because Dad ground it into my memory days and days after my bear claw buffet. To get the claws repaired is not an easy task. The bear remains de-clawed to this day.

I continued my bear attacks later on one of Ed's black bear rugs from Canada. With this attack, I felt the bear was looking at me funny, so I had to give him a piece of my mind. Again, this particular action did not get me any pats on the head, but my curious and protective qualities just get the best of me sometimes. Regardless, bear claws must be good for my teeth. Right?

After a few years of almost perfecting self-entertaining, technology improved and Mom and Dad got a little smarter. Now they have these contraptions called scat mats. Our scat mats are thin gray mats of various sizes that lie on the floor like any floor mat. When these mats are turned on, they actually provide a small shock to whomever steps on them. If you have shoes on, you will not feel the shock. On the other hand, if you have four feet and do not own any shoes, then you will definitely feel a tiny shock to your system.

Mom and Dad put these scat mats down to keep me out of my favorite places: the refrigerator, the trash cans, the bear rugs, etc. For a few years, my parents used these scat mats very successfully. Mom and Dad also enlightened other friends and family for their curious pooches. Naturally, we were never hurt by this small shock. I felt the shock once or twice and realized it was not worth the jolt of excitement. I finally decided to wait for my hard dog food instead of picking out my exact dinner from the fridge.

Luckily for me, Mom and Dad just use dummy mats that are not capable of delivering any discomfort now that Eddie and Ethan are in our family. The dummy mats look exactly like the real scat mats but simply can't provide any type of shock. Thank God! Besides, I don't have the strength to carry out my old habits anymore. Ironically, I have lost so much weight unwillingly that Mom and Dad now give me whatever extra food they can to help me gain weight. It is funny how times change.

My outrageous curiosity continued to lead to self-entertainment throughout the years, and it definitely did not end once Dad and Mom were done with school and got married in June 2002. At this point, I started referring to Crystal as Mom once she and Dad got hitched. Work, family, and lots and lots of travel took up most of their time, so I continued to keep myself busy with some of my old tricks and new tricks like fun explorations or unguided tours as I like to call them.

Where do I begin? I have escaped from our yard so many times that I could write at least four novels. Why do I continue to leave the safety of my own yard and familiar surroundings, you may ask? Well, you never know what is around the corner: a stack of sprinkle pancakes, a cute pooch, a pile of pizzas, a new squeaky stuffed animal, a fire hydrant, an enticing fat cat, or loaves of warm cheese bread. That's the point! Life should always be an adventure. If it isn't, then we are doing something wrong.

The most memorable escape I made was during a big party weekend that Mom and Dad host every year on Spring Lake. The boat traffic on Spring Lake can get pretty crazy during summer days and holiday weekends as on any public lake. Actually, many of our buddies block their schedules early in the year so they don't miss out on any of this planned craziness!

As many people (a lot of familiar and unfamiliar faces) were arriving at our house on an August weekend in 2004, the doors were opening and closing often. I decided to take it upon myself to sneak out when the door was wide open as a very, very large Igloo cooler with wheels was coming through the other way. I figured no one would miss me since the cooler was now the main entertainment.

I ran as fast as the wind. I ran up our driveway and left our yard as quickly as I could. I even wagged my tail at some of our friends driving in, but they were so preoccupied with party time that they did not think to get me back in my yard. I checked the ground in front of the neighborhood mailboxes first to make sure that neighbors did not drop a doughnut or some other tasty treat by accident when checking their mail. Then I ran out to Airline Road, which is the main street that goes through our small town. Whew! The day was busy, busy, busy with cars, trucks, and people everywhere, all over town. It was a good thing I knew to check both ways. Luckily, Dad taught me that cars can "squish" me, so I knew I better watch what I was doing. I am not a fan of Frogger, and neither is Dad.

I wandered down the sidewalk letting my sniffer take me happily along. I waved my tail to many people driving by and chased a few critters here and there. I enjoyed being out on this gorgeous day. I got to make my own decisions, and I loved it.

I explored for at least an hour it seemed. However, I don't know how much time actually passed because I don't own a watch and didn't pass any clocks along the way. I never thought telling time was important anyway because I like to believe that I am always on "island time." Too bad everyone can't be on "island time." Maybe it was two hours or maybe it was only four minutes. Either way, I loved every second I was gone adventuring!

Unfortunately, I guess all good things really do come to an end. While I was strolling down Minetta Drive watering some flowers, I heard, "Gunther, get in here!" I was busted! I looked over my shoulder and saw S-Man there. (Yes, we have a friend named S-Man. Have you noticed that many of our friends do not go by their first names? Maybe our friends should start calling me G-Dog instead of Gunther.) S-Man has been a good friend for years, so I was happy to see him even under these circumstances. Besides, he was easier on me than Dad would have been if Dad would have found me first. My adventures are always a good idea until I get home and have to face the consequences.

I jumped in S-Man's navy blue pick-up truck and headed back to my house with him. Luckily, Dad was so busy with trying to get fifty people organized to go boating for the day that he did not have time to discipline me. However, I was bummed to see that Mom had been crying while I was away on my little trip. She was afraid that I was going to get hit by a car due to the crazy amounts of traffic whizzing through the streets. She was also really stressed since there were fifty people at our house waiting on me to show up safely so they could all go party on the lake for the day. Mom just needed to relax, get a margarita, and not worry about the other party people so much. Anyway, I think everyone would have been fine never leaving the dock that day. Nicely packed coolers seem to make instant parties.

The party went off without any other hitches. My parents usually throw a good party. Just ask their friends. Forty-eight people ended up staying the night after a wild day on the lake. People slept everywhere: on the hammock, under the hammock, in the yard, in The Sand Bar, on the floor, on the boat, and upside down in their cars. Thankfully, I woke up the next day snug in my king-size bed without a headache unlike everyone else who slept at our house.

What fun I have created for myself by not allowing moss to grow underneath my paws. I decided a very long time ago to live life to the fullest each and every day. Remember to pop the bubbly over the small occasions as well as the huge celebrations and don't let a unique opportunity pass by you.

Speaking of unique opportunities, let me introduce you to my lady Memphis.

"How do I look?"

One Wild Night

Before I left my canine mom Godiva, she taught me to treat everyone with respect and remember what I stand for in every occasion that life presents to me.

Loyalty

Admiration

Bravery

Responsibility

Affection

Devotion

Originality

Reliability

I especially tried to remember these qualities when I met my beautiful Memphis in a garage on the south side of Indianapolis. Please let me explain before your mind wanders too much.

I have always been interested in finding the lovely young ladies. As I described earlier, I escaped our driveway multiple times to go looking for love, among other things. Unfortunately, I never found any permanent relationships until sweet love came knocking on my door.

Dad's Aunt Nancy called him and asked, "Is Gunther interested in meeting a hot chocolate Labrador named Memphis?" Well, she asked something like that. Anyway, I got wind of this phone call and started doing back flips and cartwheels in the other room (just making sure you are paying attention). I began working on my manners and jogging regularly with Mom to get into better shape for my needy damsel. I even started Yoga at which I was surprisingly quite good. Downward-facing dog was definitely my favorite pose.

Apparently, Mom and Dad were ready for me to meet new friends, so they arranged the first date for us. I was extremely nervous during the car ride on the way to meet Memphis. Luckily, I listened to Jimmy Buffett's *Changes in Latitudes, Changes in Attitudes* album to help keep me calm. Memphis only lived twenty minutes from me, so we were pulling into her driveway before I knew it.

Memphis made me believe in love at first sight. She was very beautiful with sparkling green eyes, shiny brown fur, a sleek body, and a kind smile. Unfortunately, I did not make her a believer. I'm sure it was due to my lack of dinner, chocolate, and flowers. Whatever it was, Memphis was *not* interested in me the first night.

Now, let me give myself a little credit here. Our first "arrangement for fun" was in her parents' garage in Indianapolis where both sets of our parents stood the whole time chatting about the weather or whatever. How many first dates beginning in the garage with the parents present lead to a second date? Alright, I think my point has been made.

Being the persevering dog that I am, I wanted a second date with Memphis. She was absolutely gorgeous, and I needed to see her again. Thankfully, our parents agreed, so we went back to Memphis' house just a few days later. Before we left, Mom brushed my teeth with one of those crazy dog toothbrushes, which tickled my gums the whole time. I really enjoyed the chicken flavored toothpaste even though my breath smelled worse afterwards.

I don't know what I did differently, but this time there were fireworks and champagne between Memphis and me! We had a romantic evening in the backyard under the stars, which was much more fun than romancing Memphis in the garage. We just ignored the fact that our parents were in the yard with us. They were obviously very excited to have grandchildren and didn't want to miss one candid moment. I supposed they would want to be in the delivery room, too. To complete our evening in the moonlight, Memphis and I exchanged happy glances and realized we didn't know when or if we would see each other again.

I found out two weeks later that Memphis was pregnant, and I was going to be a Daddy. Many nights, I laid awake thinking about our babies on the way. No, I can't tell a lie. I actually slept very well all eight weeks after we knew Memphis was pregnant. Regardless, I was very excited to meet our little ones. We only had a few weeks to register for baby gifts, but no one ever took us shopping. Oh well! What do brand-new puppies need anyway other than mommy milk, nice shoes for chewing, and lots and lots of love?

We all waited with anticipation for eight weeks and finally got a call that Memphis was healthy and had twelve beautiful puppies on May 6, 1999. Can you imagine having twelve babies at a time? Memphis was a champ, and I was so proud of her.

We drove to the south side of Indianapolis where Memphis and the pups lived, and I met our children for the very first time. What an amazing day! That was a day that I never want to forget. It was a bit overwhelming with twelve babies at once, but I wouldn't change a thing. Besides, twelve puppies were God's plan, so I would never dream of changing it. From the very first sight, I loved all of the pups like I had known them forever. I wanted to protect them with all I had and remember each moment of our first magical encounter.

I was really thankful that Memphis and her parents were taking care of the puppies. It looked like a lot of work to care for them. They were frequently attached to Memphis, drinking milk, and when they weren't drinking milk they were pooping. Puppy turds were everywhere despite Memphis' mom's attempts at keeping the backyard cleaned. Even though my babies pooped everywhere, I could not get over how cute they were. My puppies were absolutely adorable, and they were mine. I felt very happy knowing I had children.

I pray that everyone gets a chance to hold and cuddle a brand-new puppy in his or her lifetime because it is really a fantastic experience. It is even better when the puppy is your own.

Dad picked up many new puppies and put them on his lap. He enjoyed hearing their cute little squeaks. Each one of them wiggled off of his lap and clumsily ran over to Memphis for comfort. The babies stayed away from me except for one of the yellow pups who is now our Happy Dog. She actually ran over to me and bit my family jewels. At the time, I was definitely thinking this pup should have a much different name than Happy. Have you ever felt how sharp puppy teeth are? They are not comfortable on any occasion, especially if they are biting your privates. I just took it in stride and counted my blessings, all thirteen of them: Memphis plus puppies.

Much to our surprise, there were four yellow pups, four chocolate pups, and four black pups. Maybe Memphis was an accountant in her previous lifetime. All of the pups were really good looking, and we were very happy they had arrived safely. Memphis was doing well and still looked hot even after having twelve babies. I am such a lucky dog!

The next few weeks were filled with calls to check on my babies and a few visits to see how everyone was growing. Thankfully, Memphis healed up well and all of our twelve children continued to grow as expected. Finally, around week six we took one black puppy and one yellow puppy home with us. Dad wanted to get his parents a "son of a Gun," so we chose the stoutest black male in the litter. Mom always wanted a yellow Labrador, so we chose the little stinker who bit my family jewels and named her Happy. I was thrilled that I would have at least one of my children living with me. I could not wait to watch Happy grow and be with her through all of her life experiences. I was very pleased that one of my sons would be with Eric's parents, so I could also keep a close eye on him and watch him get big and strong. Best of all, I knew my puppies would help me protect those who mean the world to me.

On the first day with puppies in tow in July 1999, we took a road trip to Grand Rapids, Michigan, since Dad and I were moving there for residency. Well, technically only Dad was starting residency, but I needed to go with him for moral support. Dad's parents Ed and Anne followed us up to Michigan in a separate car, and we wanted to surprise them with both puppies once we got there.

I thought our little secret was not going to stay so secret when we stopped at Wendy's for lunch. We had the puppies in the front passenger seat of Mom's Saturn while I was on guard in the back. While everyone, except the four-legged friends, was inside having lunch, I noticed a bus full of people unloading in the parking lot. Instead of walking right into Wendy's, the entire group of people wandered over to our car to "ooh" and "ahh" over our furry four-legged creatures in the front. I knew their intentions were completely harmless, but I didn't want these total strangers to ruin our fun and sneaky surprise. If Ed saw this, he would come running out to see what these strangers were doing around my mom's car. Then the surprise would most definitely be ruined! Luckily, Dad strategically had Ed and Anne sit with their backs to the window so they wouldn't see the car from where they were sitting. Thankfully, they did not find out about their fuzzy surprises waiting for them until we reached Michigan.

After lunch, Mom got back in our car with the puppies and me, and we continued northbound on I-69 towards Michigan. We followed Ed and Anne in their Jeep and Dad in his green Chevy truck and kept our distance so they would not see the puppies in the front seat. Mom could not talk on the phone much either on the way northbound because my little son was squeaking and whining the whole time. (Hopefully, he wasn't whining because Happy was nipping at his "Kibbles and Bits," too.) Mom did not want Anne to hear a puppy squeaking in the background because she would know something was up. Finally, we arrived at Dad's house on Adams Street in Grand Rapids and got out to stretch our legs. Dad let me in the house to investigate and make sure the coast was clear as Mom covertly put the puppies on the back porch.

I got some water to drink and everyone else had iced tea to wet their whistles. Next, I led Ed and Anne through the house towards the backyard so I could do my business. Much to their surprise, there were cute little black and yellow fur balls bouncing around the back porch. To surprise us further, our fur balls had already made some pee puddles for us to step over. I guess I have some potty training to do with my children. I definitely need to work on manners with these little ones.

Ed and Anne simultaneously got tears in their eyes and huge smiles on their faces. They immediately fell in love with my offspring and learned that the tiny black one was theirs to keep. Ed and Anne named him Bear, and the rest is history. They loved Bear so much that Ed surprised Anne with a chocolate Labrador from my litter about two weeks later. They named him Moose. The funny part was that Ed and Anne already had a yellow Labrador Retriever at home, so now they had one Labrador of every color. They are going to be busy keeping up with all of their four-legged companions.

In addition to Happy, Bear, and Moose, Eric's sister took two puppies and a close friend took one more pup from my litter. These puppies became known as Bean, Poppy, and Jake. This means we have six of my twelve babies in our close family unit. I love seeing my babies, but I am glad that I have so much help to raise them. It is tough work taking care of little ones. I believe a whole village is needed to help raise children.

I lost track of Memphis and my other six children even with my best attempts to stay in touch. This makes me sad, but it is the way of life for a dog. I hope Memphis kept track of our other children. It is very important for children to have at least one of their natural parents directly involved in their lives. Anytime I see a handsome or beautiful Labrador at the park, I always wonder if he or she could be my offspring. So far I have not run into any of them, but I will never stop looking.

Life with a new puppy around took a little getting used to. I was four and a half years old when the puppies were born, so life got more exciting than I could ever imagine with Happy in our family. Happy was, and still is, full of piss and vinegar at age ten and a half. She has slowed down a tiny bit over the years, but for the most part she is still a wiggly, giggly pup at heart. Happy has definitely kept me busy all of these years, and I still love having her to pal around with and teach right from wrong. Of course, sometimes I enjoy getting into trouble more with her than teaching her good manners.

It is not unusual to find Happy and me sitting with our front legs crossed over each others, sleeping in front of the fireplace or under the disco ball. (Yes, every house we have ever owned has a disco ball in it.) We love to cuddle and lick each others' ears. It is very relaxing and reminds me of Godiva taking care of me as a new puppy. Also, I have frequent ear infections so the ear licking helps soothe my sore ears. Happy can be very helpful.

On the other hand, it is very common to find Happy sleeping in the king-size bed by herself these days while I am beside Mom and Dad every step of the way as they work around the house. Happy likes her own space and demands royal treatment 24/7, hence the name Princess Happy.

Princess Happy

Princess Happy

So how did the tiny one who nipped my family jewels end up coming to live with me forever and ever? I guess I am just lucky. I really am lucky that Happy has been with me for all of these years, but it is truly mind-blowing how two children can be raised by the same set of parents and turn out very differently. Can you relate?

Happy has a pink nose, narrow head, beautiful green eyes, and golden yellow fur. Her color fits in beautifully in the fall. Maybe she will come back in her next life as a leaf, a very energetic leaf. She is much, much thicker than a leaf currently, so we don't have to worry about confusing the two of them. On the other hand, I have a black nose, large block head, mysterious brown eyes (as Mom likes to call them), and solid black fur. Well, I do have a few white spots in my hair now, but my buddies think I look very distinguished with these age markings. As we all know, everyone is unique and has his own personal characteristics; you definitely can't judge a book by its cover.

Even though our looks are very different, Mom and Dad think we should exhibit the same morals and follow the same principles in life. Well, let me tell you, Happy and I are as different as day and night, Kiss and Jack Johnson, the sun and the moon, Guinness and Landshark Lager, and . . . I believe you get my point. We are different in so many ways that I don't know where to begin. I'll get you up to speed as quickly as I can.

Obviously, Happy is a very happy dog, and she shows you this with her whole body. When she wags her tail, her entire body wiggles like a bowl of Jell-O. Unfortunately, she doesn't care who is standing close to her when she does her wiggle dance. Sometimes she knocks Eddie, Ethan, or me over by accident when she spreads around her cheer. In the past, Happy would not be able to budge me, but with my impressive age and nice list of health problems, I am not the pillar of strength I used to be. If you are in her wiggle room, then you better watch your step closely. Besides, if Happy's body does not get you, then her tail will definitely finish you off. Her tail should be a weapon used in the armed forces. It is powerful and hurts when it whacks you. I am very surprised she has not played in the major leagues with a swing like hers. I think home runs would be Happy's specialty.

Dad gets really mad at Happy for knocking us over and attacking us with her tail. He thinks she is not very considerate. Happy tells me constantly, "I never mean to hurt anyone, but I'm happy and I want the world to know it!" She just has so much energy that she doesn't know how to control it. I say, "She's happy, so let her be." Why can't everyone just let happy people do their thing?

Let's see how Happy and I begin our days. We start the morning with stretching, Happy in the king-size bed now and me on the floor, beside the bed, due to arthritis. Anyway, we quickly head out to do our business. Every single time Happy barks like she has never barked before when she runs out the door, even if absolutely nothing is there. She will tear off, after a squirrel, a falling leaf, or thin air, barking like a wild woman! Back in my day, I chased and caught varmint after varmint, but these days I can't catch one of them even in my wildest dreams. The good side is that Happy definitely gets our little visitors running for their lives and saves face for me with them. She also saves me from many sore throats in the morning with all of her obsessive barking. I sure do miss telling the world what I think whenever I want. My time for this isn't completely gone, is it?

Happy even barks at Eddie at three in the morning when he comes into our room to sleep with Mom and Dad every night. She acts like she has never seen him before. Dad thinks Happy is afraid of her own shadow, and Mom thinks Happy has a purpose for each bark. I don't know who's correct, but I think Happy's vision is not as sharp as it used to be which leads to her neurotic barking. Well, at least we are a good team. She can hear for me, and I can see for her.

Also, I think Mom and Dad need to remember that Happy is a girl and thus has more of a need to *talk, talk, talk*. Barking is obviously her main way of communicating, so they shouldn't scold her for unnecessary barking. It is in her feminine blood. Dad, I would think that Mom would constantly remind you of this obvious fact.

Once outside, I love to explore. I feel the need to investigate every corner of our property to make sure I am not missing anything. On the contrary, exploring is not one of Happy's strong points. Is she afraid of what she will find? I know the farthest she has ever been from our house on her own will is our mailbox. I can think of many more exciting places than the mailbox to travel in this inviting world. I have been at least two miles from our house before on my unguided tours as I like to call them. Actually, I have been farther, but no one caught me. Let's hope for Mom and Dad's sake that Eddie and Ethan don't have my sneaky exploration skills. To contain my curiosity, Mom and Dad usually shut three gates so I don't escape the yard when they aren't watching. This keeps my outdoor adventures to a minimum these days.

One morning, as Dad came home from running errands, he saw Happy in the yard and decided to sneak up on her. When he scared her, she ran like a grizzly bear was chasing her. It seems as if her main goal in life is to be happy instead of being a bodyguard. I can definitely respect that. We do live in Fruitport with a yellow smiley face water tower, so it isn't all her fault.

After our morning ritual outside, watering Mom's flowers and Dad's grass, we go inside to eat some grub. Happy and I eat many excellent meals, consisting of our dog food and extra fun "little brother" treats like leftover eggs, crisp bacon, and sticky pancakes. Licking Eddie and Ethan's tiny fingers is our favorite part of meal time. I eat some of my food, and Happy eats every last lick of her bowl plus part of mine, too. Usually someone has to stop Happy from clearing out my bowl and all the cabinets during mealtime. Just teasing! Thankfully, all of her wiggles keep her weight under control.

With all of Happy's energetic qualities, you would think that she would want to be surrounded by people at all times. Actually, she is a loner unless you have food or a Frisbee in hand. I like to think of myself as a social butterfly, but my daughter Happy just isn't.

When Mom and Dad go on vacation, they usually leave us with Dad's parents Ed and Anne. We have stayed there lots over the years, so now they call their house Camp Love-A-Lot. Ed and Anne, the camp counselors, have been named BooBoo and Nana by the all the grandkids, so now I will always refer to them as BooBoo and Nana.

Since Nana is a retired third-grade teacher, she makes camp extra fun with welcome signs hanging on the front door and special treats waiting in our bowls. Nana and BooBoo always make us feel welcome. While we are at Camp Love-A-Lot, we get to play with Nana and BooBoo's doggies, Moose, Bear, and Scout. It is always fun seeing my sons and Happy's brothers, Moose and Bear, and I like to think of Scout as my girlfriend. Anyway, Happy tends to separate herself from all of us even during treat time. Nana ends up taking Happy's Milk-Bone to her in the bedroom since Happy refuses to come out and get it herself.

I haven't decided if Happy gets depressed when Mom and Dad leave or if she feels like she isn't being treated like a princess when she has to stay with the other pooches in our family. Well, at least Eddie, Ethan, and I are big advocates for Camp Love-A-Lot. Actually, Mom and Dad usually have to bribe Eddie and Ethan to come back home because they really love it there!

Happy likes to keep her space at home, too. Every time that Eddie and Ethan try to give her a hug or a kiss on the head, she jumps up and runs away. Mom usually holds her collar so Eddie and Ethan can kiss her goodnight. I treasure these times when Eddie and Ethan want to spend time with me, so I let them give me all the hugs and kisses they want. I know I won't be here forever, so I look forward to these special moments.

At night, Happy also stands by Mom and Dad's bedroom door, whining and waiting for them to open it, so she can go to bed. Instead, I follow Mom and Dad downstairs, upstairs, or wherever they go throughout the evening so I can be at their beck and call. Happy frequently says, "Gunther, I can't be at Mom and Dad's feet like you because their feet aren't big enough for one hundred seventy pounds of Labrador Retrievers." I guess she has a good point.

A time when Happy really keeps her distance is during pheasant hunting. Unfortunately, this is not ideal for effective hunting. Dad always says, "Happy hunts for herself." As soon as she hits the field, her nose is to the ground, and she is off like a horse at the Kentucky Derby. Even with Dad yelling commands, she continues to run, run, run looking for birds. She hunts very hard even though she doesn't really play by the rules.

When Happy finds a bird, she chases it until the pheasant flies into the sky. Of course, Dad is usually too far away to get a shot off because she did not hunt in close enough proximity. This is a bit frustrating when you pay twenty-five dollars a bird. If Dad is able to shoot the bird by the grace of God, Happy tracks the fallen bird and waits for help. Princess Happy does not touch the bird. She simply stands over it, wags her tail, and pants heavily until "back-up" arrives. Luckily, the "back-up" is me. I guess Happy is a "girly dog," since she does not want to have any part in touching the birds.

Speaking of "girly dog," Happy loves to smell Mom's hair when Mom gets out of the shower. When she smells Mom's fun and fragrant hair products, she wags her tail wildly and dances around like a ballerina. I think we should get Happy and Mom a spa day sometime. I think they would love this.

Happy's other extracurricular activities are Frisbee, ball, more Frisbee, and more ball. She welcomes any ages to play with her, including our one- and three-year-old brothers, our college-aged babysitter Miss Emily, and our seventy-seven-year-old uncle Ted. She has even tried to train babies to throw a ball before they can sit up, but Mom and Dad usually put a damper on this. Anyone who plays catch with Happy seems to enjoy it as much as she does. I think Happy would play Frisbee and ball every second of every day if she could.

Luckily, Happy is not picky in any way, shape, or form. Tennis balls work best, but anything round, such as an apple, a Christmas ornament, a stuffed animal, or even a small basketball, is perfect to satisfy her craving to retrieve. I have even seen her pick up Hot Wheels to entice friends and family to play, play, play.

Unfortunately, Happy does not see boating in the same light as playing Frisbee and ball. Boating is definitely not one of Happy's favorite pastimes. Princess Happy prefers to be in her castle resting rather than boating with the family. We have taken so many trips on the water that

I can not thank God enough for them, and Happy could have done without each and every one of them. On the majority of our boating excursions, Happy hunkered down by Dad's feet and stayed in a little ball. Happy enjoyed when the boat was stopped so she could swim in the lake, wherever we were, but for the most part she wanted to be home watching *Mamma Mia* on the couch.

Happy has a comical side too. She runs when she farts. She absolutely breaks out in a mad dash when she lets one slip. She can be sound asleep and off she goes like a bottle rocket when a little toot slips out. Unlike Happy, when *I* let one slip, I act as if I didn't do it and hope Ethan is close by with a poopy diaper to blame. Besides, I don't have the energy anymore to run when I fart.

Speaking of farting, Happy also holds out for soft grass to go potty. She doesn't enjoy going number two (I am trying to be more polite) in our fenced area, which consists of a driveway with low growing foliage along the sides. Instead, she waits until we go out on the other side of our house where there is a large yard full of soft and fluffy grass. She goes to the bathroom within the first minute every single time. On the other hand, I need to have privacy when I do my business, so I never potty in the middle of the yard. Preferably, I back my butt up against a tree or a fence and do my thing. I think this is the most polite thing to do. Happy definitely needs more work on her manners.

Nonetheless, Happy's manners are better than mine on some occasions. To be polite, she does not open the door until someone opens it for her. She doesn't want to barge in on anyone. Even if the door is cracked, she stands there and stares at you through the crack. She whines and says, "Please, someone help the princess." No, she really doesn't say this; but she does whine until her knight in shining armor (that's me!) opens the door for her. I have a huge head and have never been afraid to use it to get where I need to go. Whether it is writing a book or opening a door, I put my head to good use. Even if a door is completely shut, I am able to get it open most of the time if I push hard enough. If the door is slightly ajar, I go right through without a second thought. Happy needs to learn that if she wants something, she should go after it and not let any door or anything else, like wrapping paper, stand in her way.

At holidays and birthday celebrations, Happy lets wrapping paper stand in her way. Therefore, I have to open Happy's presents for her. She looks at the present in the paper and gently puts it in her mouth. Then she drops it and looks for me to tear into it for her. I don't mind this job one bit. Of course, if there are treats inside I make her share with me. If there is a stuffed toy inside with a squeaker, Happy wildly runs around squeaking the toy constantly. Thirty minutes later, if not less, she has shredded the stuffed animal, spreading all the white fuzz everywhere while looking for the squeaker. You would think she would realize the insides are the same in all of them, but she has not figured this out yet, even after ten and a half years. She definitely has a lot of heart and spirit but maybe not the most brains.

I know how to cheer Happy up anytime. This is good since I often pick on her and make her mad. One of the easiest ways to make her smile is to give her any food, but more particularly White Castle hamburgers. Dad grew up eating White Castle hamburgers, and he introduced me to these tasty treats when I was just a pup. Luckily, Dad and I lived close to a White Castle back in Bloomington for a short period of time. We visited there frequently, as you can imagine.

Even though we do not live close to a White Castle now, Dad seeks out this fine establishment whenever we travel. He doesn't forget Happy and me either. We get White Castles also, but Dad wraps our burgers in two boxes to make it a bit more challenging for us to get to our beefy treats. He thinks we enjoy our burgers a little more this way. We inhale them the second we get to them. I don't know if the extra seconds make the burgers taste better or just cause more drool to end up on the floor. I am good at puzzles, so I get my burgers out easily whereas Happy always needs help solving her puzzle. Mom usually pulls the burger out for her because Dad and I just giggle while Happy sniffs and stares at the burger boxes in front of her.

Maybe our differences boil down to one very important life experience. When Happy was one and a half years old, Mom took her to the local pet hospital to have her spayed. Happy had her normal morning routine consisting of hard dog food mixed with leftover Cheerios, Mom rushing around like a chicken with her head cut off, and a quiet car ride at five-thirty in the morning. Then out of the blue, Mom stopped by the veterinarian's office, and Happy just went along with it. Afterwards, Happy told me she thought Mom was just running errands and picking up something for her at her doctor's office. Instead, Mom dropped Happy off and left her for the entire day.

After Mom's long day of work, she drove back to pick up a little sedated and scared Happy girl. In a couple of days, Mom drove Happy to Eddie and Susie's house (Mom's parents' house in southern Indiana) so they could take care of her while Mom and Dad went on a trip.

When looking back at this decision, Mom has told us many times that she regretted leaving Happy. However, Happy had the best of care from Eddie and Susie, better known as Grandma and Grandpa. Happy definitely got more attention and tender loving care from Grandma and Grandpa than if Happy would have stayed at home with Mom. Grandparents are so good at giving that extra special attention when it is needed most.

Thankfully, I avoided any and all surgery to this day. Ever since Happy's surgery and humiliating days of wearing the lampshade around her neck to keep her from licking her incisions, she has been very afraid of going to the vet. The last time we went to the doctor together, she shook the whole time and tried to hide under the chair. As you can imagine, Happy was not very successful at hiding under the chair as an eighty-four pound Lab, but at least she tried. She is always very polite and never nips or growls. Plain and simple, she is just afraid each and every time.

I embrace going to the veterinarian's office because you never know how many hot babes you will meet there. Besides, where else is butt sniffing the norm? I like this kind of hang out.

Maybe I would have the same odd characteristics as Happy if someone had taken my "man parts" from me. Regardless of her quirkiness, I still love her, and she will always be my little girl. We should all remember that life experiences greatly shape who someone becomes, and these experiences never should be taken lightly. Never ever judge because you don't know what journey another has traveled. Just focus on each person's strengths and run with them.

Even though Happy and I have many differences, I love being her dad and constant partner in crime. Fortunately, we have learned to agree on some things, such as music that whisks us away to amazing tropical islands where we feel sand beneath our paws and are constantly on "island time." No one does this better for us than Jimmy Buffett and The Coral Reefer Band!

Canine Parrotheads

We have been Jimmy Buffett fans ever since I can remember, and his music sets the atmosphere at our house. What is not to love about him and his island music? His tunes definitely help the summer parties get sizzlin' and brighten the many, many gloomy days that Michigan has during the long winter months.

If you are not familiar with Jimmy Buffett, let me enlighten you. He is a very talented and creative singer/songwriter/musician/entrepreneur/author who takes you away to the Caribbean with his songs, restaurants, and books of margaritas, beaches, sailing, fishing, partying, and cheeseburgers. Many of his songs inspire you to follow your heart and go after your dreams no matter how big or small they are. Every time, Jimmy leaves you with a smile on your face, a song in your heart, a cheeseburger in your tummy, and a margarita or Landshark Lager in your hands.

Jimmy Buffett is very generous in raising your spirits regardless of what kind of day you are having, but he is also very generous in other capacities, such as helping those in need. I discovered that he dedicated the Labor Day show at Wrigley Field to the long-term relief efforts for the victims of Hurricane Katrina. I also recently learned that Jimmy supports other great causes and organizations, such as Save the Manatee Club, Sweet Relief Musician's Fund, and Wounded Warrior Project.

You wonder how I know all of these fun-filled facts about Jimmy Buffett? Well, my mom loves to shop as most moms do. She enjoys shopping from a catalogue from one of Jimmy's restaurants named

Margaritaville. Luckily, we are on the mailing list. Along with shopping items in this catalogue, we learn about upcoming events that Jimmy will be involved in where his good will is shown again and again.

Jimmy's fans are called Parrotheads because we actually dress up with parrot hats, coconut bras, tropical sunglasses, leis, hula skirts, and Hawaiian shirts in support of his life's work. Of course, everyone dresses in his or her own unique Parrothead way, but each outfit is just as important as the next.

Mom and Dad get all decked out in Parrothead attire anytime they see Jimmy Buffett and The Coral Reefer Band perform. Mom wears her hula skirt, coconut bra, bikini, flip-flops, lei, shell necklace, and parrot hat while Dad wears his loud Hawaiian shirt, flip-flops, lei, and a shark hat every time. Mom and Dad have traveled to a Caribbean Island called Anguilla as well as many places in the United States to see Jimmy Buffett and The Coral Reefer Band perform. They actually made it on the live DVD from Anguilla on the Dunes Preserve, and their tall and colorful shark and parrot hats made it very easy to pick them out on the video. Trust me, we have watched this video more than a few times to show Eddie and Ethan. I think I could actually run the DVD player now and point out Mom and Dad's locations all by myself.

Happy and I were lucky enough to actually tag along to one of Jimmy's infamous concerts. Even though Happy and I are pooches, our attire for the show was not lacking. We have reindeer kerchiefs and antlers for Christmas, bunny ears for Easter, and yes, Parrothead outfits for Buffett's concerts. Luckily, our Parrothead costumes get plenty of use since Mom and Dad like to host luaus. Actually, Eddie's first birthday party was a luau with over sixty-five guests. What a surprise!

Properly dressed with our leis, shell necklaces, and flip-flops (again, just checking to see if you are paying attention), we headed to Alpine Valley Music Theater in East Troy, Wisconsin. We rode in the

back of the Suburban while listening to Mom and Dad sing Jimmy
Buffett songs the entire drive from Fruitport. If only Mom and Dad
did not sing every single word to every single song. I wanted to ask,
"Hey, Mom and Dad, who sings these songs?" When they responded,
"Jimmy Buffett," then I could tell them, "Good, let's keep it this way."
Although, I didn't say this because I didn't want to hurt their feelings.

We arrived at the music theater hours before the show started so
we could tailgate and get geared up for a great night. We brought Red
Stripe, margaritas, chips and salsa, and cheeseburgers to fill our tummies
before the show. Happy and I both have seizures periodically. We are
not allowed to have any beer or margaritas because alcohol lowers our
seizure threshold and causes us to have seizures more frequently. We
definitely want to avoid seizures at any cost so no toddies for us. This
way there were more beverages for Mom and Dad, and I know they
weren't disappointed. On the yummy side of things, Happy and I both
enjoyed cheeseburgers before the concert.

We strolled up and down many aisles of parked cars with people
partying everywhere. Parrotheads know how to have fun! Grills,
margarita machines, large parrot costumes, cars decorated like shark
fins, corn hole games, and dancing hula girls surrounded us. I liked
meeting all of our new Parrothead friends. I ran up to every stranger I
could find and made sure he or she was my best friend before I trotted
over to another fan. Happy, on the other hand, was not too sure about
all of these new people in strange outfits petting and talking to her.
If they would have thrown her a Frisbee she would have changed her
mind, but no such luck that day. People were busy downing adult
beverages instead of playing Frisbee with the kids. We didn't have time
to play Frisbee anyway because we had too many new people to meet
before the show started.

Happy and I were not allowed into the concert venue even though we thought Jimmy would not mind. Mom and Dad were unable to successfully disguise us well enough to sneak us past security at the entrance gates. I've heard it is hard enough to sneak in a beer much less two full-grown Labrador Retrievers. Happy and I were bummed, but we decided to play in the Suburban while Mom and Dad were in the show. Dad left us lots of cold water and snacks to enjoy while we listened to the music from the S.U.V. The temperature outside was perfect for us to stay in the Suburban with the windows cracked during the concert. Mom even took off our leis and necklaces so we would not choke ourselves accidentally. Mom had to make sure her kiddos were safe. By the way, this concert was before Eddie and Ethan were born. See how much attention we used to get. We used to go many, many thrilling places.

Happy and I were able to listen to the exciting music from the parking lot. My favorite instrument is the steel drum which we heard frequently throughout the evening. The music created by the steel drums takes me on a direct flight somewhere sunny, warm, and south every time.

About halfway through the concert, when Jimmy was singing "Son of a Son of a Sailor," Happy and I fell asleep with full bellies. Mom and Dad found us after the show spooning and snoring. Besides, whenever we are among Parrotheads, we are among friends so we could take the night off from being bodyguards. Luckily, with our early evening snooze, we were all rested up for the post-show tailgating. We had an exciting evening taking a musical voyage through the islands with Jimmy Buffett and The Coral Reefer Band.

As a tribute to Jimmy Buffett, we have a little bar at our house that we named The Sand Bar. Actually, it used to be a small guest house off the garage where the previous owners' grandchildren slept. Once we moved in, Mom and Dad thought a party room would be more useful and fun especially since they didn't have any babies yet.

Dad never does anything on a small scale, so he decided to make it a true sand bar and add lots of sand. Oh yes, Mom and Dad put tarps down over the existing carpet and unloaded two tons of sand in there. Happy and I supervised throughout the project and gave our approval by sleeping long hours with the cool sand on our bellies.

Dad proceeded to make a bamboo bar and install a kegerator so we could always have beer on tap during the warm summer months. Again, I do not get to partake in this, but many of Mom and Dad's friends really enjoy this added feature. We have multiple items from Jimmy Buffett's Margaritaville on the wall as well as items from previous concerts. Any fun and tropical decoration is allowed in The Sand Bar. Dad even has a beer collection from all over the world hanging from the ceiling. Happy and I have spent many late nights in The Sand Bar playing and watching Mom, Dad, and all of their buddies get funnier as the nights progress. Happy and I never get tired of relaxing with Mom and Dad there. As our neighbor Mr. O. says, "Nothing but fun in The Sand Bar." Too bad I don't have opposable thumbs because I would be an awesome bartender and a big helper during parties.

As you can see, Jimmy Buffett brings smiles to Parrotheads all over the world. I hope to follow in his footsteps. Many of Jimmy's footsteps are made on his boat or while hanging ten on his surfboard. Thinking of Jimmy Buffett, The Sand Bar, and surfing, I long to be on the water. Boating is definitely a passion in my life as well as Mom and Dad's.

Captain Gunther

Captain Gunther

If I had to work, I would definitely drive a boat to make a living. I absolutely love boating whether it is fishing, sailing, joy riding, wakeboarding, or water skiing. It doesn't matter. Put me on a boat, and you will see a very content poochie pooch.

We have had many fun times boating whether it be on Spring Lake, Lake Michigan, Gun Lake, or any other body of water. Mom and Dad even named their thirty-two foot Carver Montego after Happy and me. It is named *Ruffin' It*, and One Particular Harbor is the name of our home port. (Are you paying attention, Jimmy Buffett fans?) Mom and Dad also had a graphic designer make a logo with a picture of Happy and me for the transom of our boat.

Often times, our wagging tails bring smiles to other boaters when they see us on *Ruffin' It*. It is amazing how many people on the water are dog lovers. Actually, Happy and I have made it easier for Mom and Dad to meet people in various marinas on our boating adventures. Well, Mom and Dad usually don't need help meeting people, but we like to think we help them out any way we can.

We have taken short boat rides to Hanky Pank Cove and Old Boys' Brewhouse on Spring Lake where we live. We have also ventured much farther, such as across Lake Michigan to Milwaukee. Of course, with all of these excursions, many memorable things happen that keep us barking about the trips for years.

Speaking of Hanky Pank Cove, Dad and I really enjoy any trip to this particular inlet on our lake. For a little history, Hanky Pank Cove is a bayou on Spring Lake, Michigan, known for people tying their boats together on hot summer weekends and holidays to party. And I mean party! (Hanky Pank Cove isn't the official name for the cove, but Hanky Pank sounds much more fun than the bayou's actual name. It has been referred to as Hanky Pank Cove for years and years, so we'll keep it this way.) As you can imagine, lots of sunbathing, hula hooping, swimming, and stupid human tricks occur during time spent at Hanky Pank Cove. For the biggest party weekends on the lake, it is very common to find over five hundred boats rafted together in this inlet. There is definitely some hanky panky that occurs in Hanky Pank Cove.

On a hot summer weekend in August 2004, Mom and Dad happened to be hanging out at Hanky Pank Cove with a very large group of friends. Naturally, Happy and I were in tow. Happy and I were dressed up as usual in funny hats and colorful bead necklaces. We were all having a great time relaxing in the sunshine, listening to some Jimmy Buffett tunes, and watching people get drinks from the "party ball." The "party ball" is a big plastic ball that holds your favorite beverage with a pump on top to make your desired drink easily accessible. (Sometimes too accessible.)

I also watched hula hooping contests on the bow of our boat while other friends stared at tiny bikinis spread throughout the cove. Obviously, I was watching the hula hooping contest and nothing else. The margaritas were flowing, the guacamole was disappearing, and Happy and I were catching random chips in mid-air. To top it off, the cooler appeared to have a hole in it, and life was good!

I decided it was time to take a swim. I asked Happy to go with me, but she told me that she was just going to relax in the sunshine. I was hot and had to pee like a racehorse. I tend to get hotter than Happy quicker because my shiny black fur attracts the heat more intensely than her golden yellow fur. I wasn't going to waste any more time.

I jumped up from my cushy seat in the stern of *Ruffin' It* and dove into the refreshing water. I don't think anyone noticed for quite a while. The water felt perfect! It was exactly what I needed until I noticed boats coming right at me as I was swimming across the cove. Boats aren't supposed to cause a wake when motoring in the cove, so I should have had plenty of time to swim away from approaching boats without getting hurt. However, as we all know, everyone doesn't always follow the rules. Since I soon realized that this day may have been my last, I decided right then and there to make this adventure well worth it.

Within a short period of time, however, I heard Mom yell, "Oh No! Gun is in the water. What are we going to do? *Eric, go get him!*" By this time, I was halfway to shore; I was going to keep swimming in this direction to get my curious paws on land. I had to dodge jet skis, wakeboard boats, cabin cruisers, canoes, kayaks, and party floats all dancing around the inlet, but I made it with no problems. For most of my life, I have been a very strong and efficient swimmer, so I figured my excellent swimming skills would get me where I needed to go.

I never looked back and started peeing on all kinds of new territory once I reached land. Anything I could find was fair game; as a dog, the world is my urinal. I was ready to play, play, play! I forgot to mention that many party goers were whistling and yelling at me to board their boats when I was swimming across the cove. Too bad no one followed me to shore so I would have a buddy to explore with on land.

Everything smelled good since this was new territory for me. I had very big plans for the afternoon, that is until Dad showed up unexpectedly just minutes after I relieved myself. I knew I was in big trouble then! He was glad I was safe, but he was worried because he still had to get us back across the cove in one piece. Have you seen the size of some of these boat propellers? Even the smallest ones can cause major bodily harm. Never get in the way of one of these things. Luckily, when Dad found me, he just gave me a look, which told me I better get back to *Ruffin' It* immediately! I guess my punishment could have been much worse. Off we went, swimming very defensively through the boat traffic; eventually, we arrived safely back at the boat just like I had planned.

Unfortunately, once we were back on *Ruffin' It*, Mom gave me a piece of her mind. What was she thinking? I am a dog, and I like to swim. Besides, I can't watch hula hoopers all day. I am glad that Mom didn't have a heart attack and that Dad and I made it back in one piece. However, I wish that my adventure could have lasted longer.

Dad and I were tired and out of breath from our long swim, but we were still in fine shape to continue our lazy afternoon of playing in Hanky Pank Cove on a hot summer day. Maybe I would have met my next Memphis, the mother of my children, if I would have had a little more time to explore. The good thing is that Mom was no longer mad at me after she had a drink from the "party ball." The party was back on again! I spent the remainder of the afternoon resting my head on a smiley face life preserver dreaming about my adventures earlier that day.

Hanky Pank Cove is not the only place to explore on Spring Lake. Another favorite spot of mine, located on the west end of Spring Lake, is Old Boys' Brewhouse. It is a local brewpub named after Old Boy, a chocolate Labrador Retriever who passed away a few years ago. He was so inspiring to all who knew him that his family opened a restaurant devoted to doggies and beer. The walls are filled with pictures of doggies from all over the country whose parents want their dogs to be represented here with the other happy pooches on the wall. (Mom and Dad still haven't gotten my picture up there yet. We need to work on this.)

The menus at Old Boys' Brewhouse are shaped like different doggy needs and desires like bowls, bones, mailmen, and fire hydrants. Most of the items on the menu have fun doggy names like Spot's Spiffy Nachos, Rufus' Rockin' Wings, and Rover Waggin' Red. Funny shirts like "Need a bone?" are for sale along with fresh homemade doggy treats. It is great that I can read, so I can understand the hilarious tee shirts and order off the menu. No, I don't actually get to order off the menu right now. However, I will know exactly what I want when Mom and Dad come around on this issue.

Dogs are welcome next to the deck at Old Boys' Brewhouse when the weather cooperates. While sitting close to Mom and Dad, Happy wants to snag table scraps while I hope to meet more and more friends. Naturally, I desire a few table scraps, too. Mom and Dad are even members of the Dog House Mug Club, so they get their beverages in fun mugs with each meal. As you can see, it is actually fun to be in the dog house at this restaurant.

Spring Lake is exciting, but Happy and I have ventured much farther than Spring Lake on the water with Mom and Dad. Saugatuck, Michigan, comes to mind and is a great destination we have floated to many times over the years. It is about three hours by boat from our dock on Spring Lake to the dock at Sergeant Marina where we like to stay. I really like the lush green park adjacent to the marina where I can mark my territory as countless other doggies have done. Also, Happy can chase geese any time of day here. Saugatuck is filled with shops, bars, art galleries, marinas, beaches, and a beautiful lighthouse; our family visits Saugatuck for all the town has to offer.

During the summer of 2005, we took a trip to Saugatuck for a little rest and relaxation. Again, this was pre-Eddie and Ethan so travels were much easier and more frequent those days. We took *Ruffin' It* across

Spring Lake, through the channel, past the Grand Haven Lighthouse, and out onto Lake Michigan. Lake Michigan is a majestically inviting, seemingly endless body of water that should be on everyone's travel plans at some point in time. I remember I sat in the backseat as usual, for the entire trip, so the sunshine could heat my bones. I sniffed the air ninety miles a minute as the boat glided through the water. It is not uncommon for Mom and Dad to find me on the stern of the boat with my paws hanging over the side, and ears flapping in the wind, enjoying the world passing me by. Now this is living! Happy stayed under the helm beside Dad's feet so she could feel secure as possible until she could get back to land. The trip was uneventful in terms of the weather—seventy-five degrees temperature and plentiful sunshine—with waves of one foot or less. It was an absolutely perfect summer day to go boating.

Once we settled into Sergeant Marina, we decided to explore our destination of Saugatuck. First, we played Frisbee in the park to help all of us burn a little energy before strolling through Saugatuck's lively streets. Then, the four of us walked through the quaint town lined with cute shops, intriguing galleries, fun bars, and amazing smelling restaurants. I didn't miss a beat weaving in and out of the oodles and oodles of people lining the streets on a busy summer afternoon. Saugatuck is a large tourist destination in the summer with its absolutely beautiful location on Lake Michigan. I was happy to interact with all of these new friends whereas Happy was bothered by the large numbers of people walking close to her. I approached as many people as I could, wagged my tail, and made them smile before I moved on to my next possible buddies. My philosophy: *make the world better one wag at a time!*

Unfortunately, we had to stay outside while Mom and Dad were shopping. Thankfully, we were rewarded well with a piece of doggy pizza from Decadent Dogs in the heart of the Saugatuck shopping area once

Mom and Dad's afternoon activities were complete. The pizza made the wait well worth it. Happy and I even tried on Doggles, dog sunglasses with a strap around the head to keep them in place. I could have easily adjusted to wearing Doggles on an everyday basis, but Happy took hers off right away; Mom and Dad didn't buy them for us.

We finished our lazy afternoon by heading back to the boat and taking a nap in the main cabin. Happy and I slept in one of the boat beds, but we had to cuddle close because it was not our usual king-size mattress. Eventually, Happy and I got hot and jumped down to take turns sitting in front of the air conditioner while our parents snoozed the afternoon away.

Everyone was so comfy that all four of us slept until the sun had set and the stars were out to play. We missed the sunset, nice restaurant for dinner (well, we were going to try and convince Mom and Dad to take us with them), and a late round of Frisbee in the park. Once we woke up, Mom hurriedly got ready for late-night food while Dad took Happy and me out to do our business. Sadly, they didn't take us along for dinner even after all of our subliminal hints. I guess the bowls of dog food on the floor were obvious clues.

Since they got such a late start, Mom and Dad stayed out late dancing the night away while Happy and I just chilled out in the main cabin. The cabin door was locked at the top of the stairs so we wouldn't go exploring, but the hatch was still open so we would get some fresh air throughout the evening.

Out of nowhere, from a deep sleep, Happy stood up and said, "I gotta go!" Before I knew it, she bounced up the steps, did a three-foot vertical jump through the open hatch, and sprang out of the cabin onto the main deck. She hopped onto the dock and ran to the nearest grassy spot. Apparently, she really did have to go. Happy certainly has a curious side to her, so she started wandering and using her sniffer to check out absolutely everything in the park. I watched the whole time from a window in the galley.

Finally, she wanted to come back and board *Ruffin' It*, however, she didn't know which boat was hers. Happy frantically barked and barked, but I didn't respond. I couldn't help but laugh because she had no idea which boat was ours even though she had ridden on it many, many times. She really is blonde! I wasn't trying to be mean. I was simply trying to teach her a lesson and get a giggle out of it at the same time. She should have come right back to the boat when she was done with her business. Of course, I would have done the same thing she did, but I didn't want Happy strolling the streets by herself without me to back her up. I would have followed her, but I've never had a three-foot vertical jump in me. Sorry, Happy.

Luckily, Mom and Dad came home a few minutes after Happy's escape from *Ruffin' It*. They boarded the boat and found me down below like the good puppy that I am. Immediately, Mom noticed Happy was nowhere on the boat. Mom frantically yelled, *"Eric, someone stole Happy!"* They both noticed the door was still shut and locked like they left it before they went out for the night, but Dad knew there had to be some other explanation. Dad looked around again and said, "Crystal, no one stole Happy! Just calm down so we can find her. Regardless, someone would have stolen Gunther before they would have stolen Happy."

Dad is always teasing Mom that I am a better and cooler dog than Happy. Mom thinks we are equally cool. Mom shot Dad an evil look through her tear-glazed brown eyes. I started to feel bad because I could have helped Happy get back to our boat and avoid this whole situation, but I wanted her to learn her lesson.

Mom and Dad hopped onto the dock and went looking for Happy. Seconds later, they found Happy lying down in front of another cabin cruiser a couple slips down from us. When she heard Mom and Dad, she jumped up, sprinted to them, and wagged her tail like she had never wagged it before! Happy said, "Thank you! Thank you! Thank you for coming home so soon! I promise I will never jump ship again without you." It sounded like, "*Bark! Bark! Very anxious bark!*" to Mom and Dad, but I think they understood what she was telling them.

We all slept very well that night following the evening's excitement. The next morning was Father's Day. Early in the morning, I sneaked out of the cabin onto the main deck. I sprang up onto the cushy seats, rested with my paws hanging over the stern, and held my head high in the air smelling the freshness all around. Once everyone was awake, I got another piece of pizza from Decadent Dogs, and Dad got a beer at a restaurant/bar called Wally's to celebrate what great Daddies we are.

To continue a perfect Father's Day, we stopped at a swim-up beach on our journey back to Spring Lake. Once the anchor was in place, all four of us swam to shore. The beach was very private and had a creek running through it. The beaches along Lake Michigan are absolutely pristine and make you feel like you are in the Caribbean except, of course, in the middle of winter. Many of the beaches are lined with sand dunes which make for additional adventure and beauty. Happy and I splashed, ran, played as hard as we could, and cooled off in the fresh water during our fun afternoon. We love having easy access to a huge body of fresh water, and it's great not having to worry about sharks. Happy and I also really appreciate the lack of salt in Lake Michigan. We prefer to be unsalty dogs.

We played for a couple of hours in the sun. Eventually, Happy and I had to relieve ourselves, so we hiked up the sand dunes. As you already know, Happy loves to potty in wide-open places, and I enjoy a little privacy. There was not a lot of activity in the sand dunes that day; I decided to take care of business. After Happy and I made our deposits, Mom came along with her little bag to carry our treats back to the boat. The comical part is that our doggie doo started rolling down the sand dunes as Mom and Dad were trying to scoop it, so they had to chase it. This led to everyone laughing hysterically and falling in the sand. Finally, Mom and Dad captured their targets and all of us continued on with our Sunday Fun-Day.

We ended up swimming back to the boat after a few more minutes on the beach and caught our breath lying in the sunshine on the bow of *Ruffin' It*. After a few snacks, we decided it was time to get home. Once we were underway, Dad and I said, "Hey, everyone, let's go fishing on the way home." Well, that is what it sounded like when Dad said it. When I spoke, it sounded more like, "*Bark! Bark! Super happy bark!*" but they obviously got my message. Mom and Happy looked at us and started helping with setting lines and driving the boat. We definitely enjoy fishing together as a family. We think the family who goes fishing together stays together, that is after the initial discussions are worked through. Let me explain.

Dad and I have always loved to fish. To be honest with you, I don't know if Happy even cares to go fishing. Mom likes to "go catching" because she feels like she should be home getting stuff done when she is "just fishing." However, if she is catching, then she feels productive. You would think after seven and a half years of marriage Mom would have learned that angling is not about the catch. Instead, fishing is about the people you share your day with and the stories that make up your trip.

Speaking of learning, there is so much to learn about fishing. When Mom and Dad first ventured out on Lake Michigan together in our thirty-two foot Carver Montego, I overheard many discussions that went something like this: "Crystal, keep the boat straight while driving. You are getting the lines tangled up!" said Dad. Mom *quickly* replied, "I *am* keeping the boat straight. I can't help that you put out too many lines. Of course, they are going to get tangled!"

These little conversations inevitably ended when a big salmon jumped on their hooks and came to visit them in the boat. Mom and Dad were both so excited about the salmon that they always forgot about their heated discussions. Sometimes I think fish are just being polite to fishermen and fisherwomen by grabbing onto their hooks so the fishing parties involved will stop bickering over the logistics. I must admit that Mom has come a long way. She still likes to "go catching," but at least she is very helpful with setting lines, driving the boat correctly, and most importantly cooking the fish. When Dad tries to get her to filet them, she says, "I can't do everything on this boat."

Even though there is so much research on fishing, Mom still says, "I think it is all luck, and we might as well fish with hot dogs." "Do hot dogs work?" you ask. Funny thing is we can't seem to remember to bring hot dogs with us to test Mom's theory, but we have a suspicion she is totally wrong. Regardless, I don't care what we use as bait as long as we catch some type of underwater creature.

On our relaxing summer afternoon of Father's Day fishing, the lines were all set with wire divers at one hundred twenty feet back and high divers at one hundred sixty feet back. The downriggers were set between thirty-five and fifty-five feet down with some lures that have interesting names like Double Orange Crush Magnum, Michael Jackson, Pickled Sunshine, Mixed Veggies, Flounder Pounder, Meat Rig, Monkey Puke, Lemon Ice, and Kevorkian. The Depth Raider showed the water temperature was forty-seven degrees at seventy feet deep.

I told you there is a lot to learn about big water fishing, and as you can see I have learned my fair share by being Captain Gunther all of these years. We actually learn new things each time we go out on the boat, which is why it is extremely exciting and challenging. The best part of every trip is that we never know what we are going to pull out of the mysterious waters of Lake Michigan.

While fishing, I always stay in the stern close to the fishing poles so I can help when there is a fish on the line. Soon after we started fishing, Dad yelled, *"Fish on! Come on, Crystal, you can get him!"* The whole time, I stood there patiently in case Mom needed back up. Mom reeled and reeled and reeled while her pole rested in her fish fighting belt. A fish fighting belt is a belt (obviously) that has a small hole on the front where the fishing rod sits so it doesn't dig into the angler's body while reeling in the fish. I recommend for all anglers, especially Mommy anglers, to have these. It makes this sport more fun and comfy for them, especially when they are fighting the catch of the day for a long time. What a thoughtful and functional present for any time of the year!

The shiny silver salmon jumped sporadically out of the blue waters of Lake Michigan to show us his mighty size. Each time Mom reeled it closer, the salmon took line and tried to get farther from the boat. As this monster fish kept challenging Mom more and more, she said, "######, ******, ###****!" I am not allowed to repeat these choice words, but I think you get the point. She is not allowed to say these words anymore because of Eddie and Ethan's little ears.

After ten minutes of fighting the salmon, it had finally tired out, so she was able to reel him close to the stern of the boat. Can you imagine swimming away from a thirteen thousand pound boat while hooked on a twenty-five pound test line with a one inch treble hook jammed in your mouth? Me either! Fish are amazing creatures. I have a lot of respect for these animals. I know I couldn't do what they do.

Dad was driving the boat during all of this excitement. I should have offered my boat driving services, but I didn't want to miss any action. When the fish was close enough, Dad ran back and grabbed the net. He scooped up the fish with no struggles at all to show Mom that she had caught a beautiful king salmon. Mom was out of breath and her scrawny arms were very tired from fighting the salmon, so I knew she was happy to have her catch completed. I licked the fish to make sure it was safe for my family to eat. Luckily, Dad always lets me play with the catch of the day before it goes in the cooler.

Whether it is fishing on Spring Lake, Gun Lake, Lake Michigan, or Grandpa and Grandma's lake in Indiana, I enjoy every minute. As most of us know, fishing is not about how many fish we catch. To me, it is about spending time with my favorite people and enjoying Mother Nature.

These days, however, it is hard for me to go fishing. My balance is not what it used to be, so standing on the boat when it is underway is extremely difficult. Sometimes Dad picks me up and lays me in the boat so the two of us can go fishing in our sixteen-foot Sea Nymph right off of our dock. I usually sleep the whole time now, as compared to years ago when I wouldn't blink an eye because I was afraid I might miss something. It is funny how time takes its toll on our bodies and energy levels. I can still do small boat trips, and I appreciate any boat trip at all. However, memories will be the closest I can get anymore to long boating adventures on Lake Michigan.

My best memory of our biggest boating trip on Lake Michigan was in June 2005 (pre-Eddie and Ethan days). Mom, Dad, Happy, and I ventured across Lake Michigan to Milwaukee. If you look at Michigan and Wisconsin on a map, you will see that Lake Michigan separates the two states. If you look closer, Grand Haven, Michigan, and Milwaukee, Wisconsin, are across from each other; we decided to head west to Milwaukee.

On the way west across the big lake, the water was mostly calm and perfect. We even stopped halfway across to take a family swim. How awesome! The only not-so-awesome part was that we couldn't get *Ruffin' It* to start right away once our little swim was complete. We wanted to get to Milwaukee before sunset since we knew it would be much easier to navigate for the first time in the daylight. Mom almost flipped out, and Dad kept his calm the entire time. He always says, "We are problem solvers. We can always figure out an answer." Good thing he actually practices what he preaches. Captain Daddy got the boat to kickin' in no time, and off we continued to Milwaukee.

We arrived safely before sunset with our adventure hats in place. I love exploring new territory, and exploring is exactly what I did. Thankfully for Mom and Dad, I decided to avoid unguided tours in this new town. Instead, I explored every nook and cranny of a huge park located next to the marina with Mom and Dad supervising the entire time. We had picnics, chased Dad's flip-flops, smelled many fresh and exciting scents, and met new friends. We even had our new friends throwing Dad's flip-flops so they could play with us. Why flip-flops? We had to play catch with Dad's flip-flops because Mom and Dad forgot to pack our Frisbees. This cracks me up because they *never ever* forget to pack the cooler. It is always other items like my Frisbee, their toothbrushes, or paper towels, but never the cooler. It is funny how human brains work. The grass at the park was extremely soft on our paws and the shade under the huge trees felt very refreshing after retrieving Dad's flip-flops for long periods of time on the hot summer days.

Happy and I stayed on *Ruffin' It* at the South Shore Yacht Club protecting our boat while Mom and Dad went to explore Milwaukee. Luckily, Happy didn't escape this time because Mom and Dad closed the hatch, locked the door, and turned on the air conditioning.

Our stay in Milwaukee went way too quickly. As we all know, time flies when you're having fun. To add to our trip fun meter, some of our good friends were at the same marina on their sailboat named *Cheers* preparing to sail in the Queen's Cup. The Queen's Cup is an overnight sailboat race across Lake Michigan held by South Shore Yacht Club. Approximately eighty-eight miles separate the starting harbor to the finishing harbor. The destination alternates each year between Muskegon, Michigan, and Grand Haven, Michigan.

We waited to leave the marina after all of the participating sailboats hoisted their sails and danced across the lake into the horizon. The colors were absolutely amazing! Yes, most dogs are color blind. For some reason, I am not. I am blessed with the ability to see all things bright and beautiful.

We ventured towards home with hopes of an easy motor back across the lake once the sailboats were underway with the wind carrying them towards the finish line. We passed through the sailboats and enjoyed the beauty of the skyline with hundreds of sails surrounding us. We felt bad motoring across the lake, passing the spectacular sailboats with only the wind as their engines. However, we were glad to know that we would be home in a few hours compared to twelve hours or so for the sailboats.

It was now almost dark. Instead of an easy drive home, an unexpected storm arose and waves rose to approximately six feet. Happy definitely was not happy with this! She stayed down below in the cabin and hunkered down. Dishes fell out of cabinets, pictures came off the cabin walls, the hatch flew off the front, and our spotlight broke off the bow of the boat. Mom even started to get a little sea sick. I held on as best as I could even though I kept falling from side to side in the main cabin. Thank God I was much younger then because I know there is no way my body could handle that kind of stress again.

After being stuck in this crazy storm for longer than I wanted, we saw the Grand Haven Lighthouse in the distance telling us home was getting closer and closer. Lighthouses really give boaters a strong sense of security. This trip could have turned out much differently, but it didn't. Thankfully, my affinity for boating remains.

To celebrate our safe return home, we docked *Ruffin' It* in Grand Haven along the concrete wall that lines the channel so Mom and Dad could grab carry-out food from Snug Harbor. We used many large fenders to keep our boat from banging against the concrete as the water continued to dance carelessly beneath us. Boating always makes me hungry, especially when we have to "ruff it" through a storm. The seafood nachos at Snug Harbor are out of this world! We devoured our nachos as we watched the majestic musical fountain overlooking the channel that people from all over come to enjoy. Once the fountain was done dancing and singing, I fell asleep to the hum of the boat as Captain Dad safely drove us all the way back to our dock on Spring Lake.

Have I proven to you my true love for the water? If you ever have a chance to take a boat ride, live on the water, be a captain, or be a fish for the day, *seize the opportunity*! There is something so magical about the water that it gives me a feeling of Pura Vida.

Pura Vida

Pura Vida is Spanish for pure life and has many special meanings for our family. Mom and Dad were first introduced to Pura Vida by Costa Ricans, also known as Ticos, when they visited Costa Rica. Costa Rica's country motto is Pura Vida which means more than pure life to the Ticos and those who fall in love with this beautiful place while visiting. Pura Vida tells all of us that life is short, so spread happiness while we are here and make every day count. It was very apparent to Mom and Dad that the way of Ticos really defined a pure life. I wonder if world peace could truly be possible if every country had a motto similar to Pura Vida.

My parents had an amazing time in Costa Rica and have really tried to live Pura Vida like the Ticos ever since. Obviously, my parents brought this Costa Rican thinking home and have tried to teach all of us about it. I almost feel as if I have been to Costa Rica due to the pictures of Macaws, Howler Monkeys, and brightly colored frogs I've seen, and the endless stories of adventure, beauty, and fun I've heard. Maybe I can see Costa Rica myself one day. If I live a pure life and am honest in everything I do, hopefully I will be graced to see Costa Rica from the best view: from up above.

To continue the positive energy of Pura Vida, Mom and Dad had a house built and named it Pura Vida. Currently, our Pura Vida home is not in Costa Rica, but in Ludington, Michigan, on a high bluff overlooking Lake Michigan. The view is absolutely breathtaking! Mom and Dad had this house built for a real estate investment as well as a super-fun getaway. Platinum Builders started building Pura Vida in January 2009 and completed it a few months later so we could enjoy it throughout the summer. During the construction process, as you can imagine, Dad was working extra shifts and Eddie and Ethan were working Mom overtime at home. Any extra time off Mom and Dad had was consumed with driving to and from meetings with builders, looking at inventory at the local hardware stores, and visiting the job site where Pura Vida was coming to life.

Unfortunately, I continued having more and more accidents in the house during the building process. They most likely happened because Mom and Dad were not home as often to let me out as frequently as I needed. I was growing older, and my bladder was getting weaker. My parents seemed to get more and more frustrated with me after accidents because they just didn't need another thing on their plates to handle. I hated to disappoint them, but I just couldn't help it.

At least in the midst of my unplanned bladder craziness, there was an extremely comical element. Every time I had an accident in the house, it was unexpected for everyone, including my parents and me. When my fire hose started spraying, Mom and Dad jumped up and grabbed anything close by to help reduce the mess. They have hastily picked up sand pails, shape sorters, Halloween treat baskets, and diapers to catch my flow. Dad has even chased me with a Tonka dump truck to keep my surprises from landing on the carpet. Even though I am mad at myself for having these accidents, my parents' desperate actions bring a little smile to my face every time. I guess every dark cloud really does have a silver lining.

I think you get my point that Mom and Dad did not have much additional time for extracurricular family activities, such as fishing, hunting, and date nights during the creation of Pura Vida. Even though my health has not been able to support hiking, running, and swimming lately, I still miss these times together as a family.

Regarding date nights, I wish Mom and Dad would have left the boys with Happy and me periodically. Nana Dog in Peter Pan used to babysit Wendy, Michael, and John while Mother and Father Darling went to dinner. I certainly don't understand why my parents never left Eddie and Ethan with Happy and me. We would have had so much fun! I also think we would have done a better job than Nana Dog because there would be a 1:1 ratio for us instead of a 1:3 ratio as there was with Nana Dog.

I just wish I could have helped Mom and Dad a little more throughout the busy construction period. At least I always played with Eddie and Ethan as much as possible to help Mom and Dad get a few things done around the house.

I still play with Eddie and Ethan as much as I can. I love to smell scratch and sniff books, lick plastic food at Elmo's Restaurant, carry stuffed animals around the house, and listen to books about Clifford the Big Red Dog. (I would really like to meet Clifford one day. He seems like a nice pooch with great manners.) Naturally, my favorite playtime is cuddling with Eddie and Ethan when they are sleepy and reading books with Mom and Dad. However, sometimes I get into trouble because I actually lie down on top of the bedtime books. Eddie gets frustrated with me when I do this because he is not big enough to pull the books out from underneath me yet. Regardless, I don't want to miss a minute with Eddie and Ethan and know I won't if I hold their story books hostage.

Luckily, Pura Vida turned out exactly as we hoped. It definitely emanates the true meaning of Pura Vida from every corner and spreads cheer to everyone who visits. We feel like we are on vacation whenever we spend time there. Pura Vida was completed in June 2009, and we had a Disco 'til Dawn party to start the house off right. Yes, Pura Vida has a disco room. Shouldn't every house have one?

The summer went quickly as we made many trips to visit the house. Thankfully, Pura Vida is only a short nap away from our house in Fruitport. With each visit, we wanted to stay longer but never could. Luckily, Dad had vacation time later in the year, so we got to spend multiple days at Pura Vida together as a family. It was magical being at Pura Vida for more than a couple of days at a time.

Even with a brand-new house, there were still many things to work on, especially outside. We did all kinds of yard work during our vacation. Every time Mom and Dad were outside working, whether gardening, raking, mowing, weeding, or packing the car, I was right there to help any way I could! I'm always on duty when there is work to be done.

Speaking of work, Dad installed a fence at Pura Vida to keep us from falling over the bluff. While Dad was working, I followed his every step as always. Well, almost every step. He didn't fall, but I did. One minute I was walking behind him, helping like I have always done. Next thing I knew, I was uncontrollably rolling down the steep bluff. Seconds later, my falling was immediately stopped by the only tree sticking out of the side of our bluff. I yelled, *"Ouch!"* when I rolled into the tree, but I don't think anyone heard me. This really hurt!

Once I had time to assess the damage, I realized that I had no broken bones and was going to be just fine. However, I could not get up for the life of me. I tried rolling over but couldn't due to the steepness of the bluff. I tried barking for help, but I was so out of breath and nervous from my fall that I couldn't muster up enough energy to make a decent bark. I had no idea what I was going to do. Luckily, Dad quickly noticed that his shadow was missing. He cautiously climbed down the bluff and slowly carried me back up one steady step at a time. BooBoo was at the top and safely helped lift me up and over the edge back to level ground.

I do not recommend using this path to get to our private and sandy beach. I think everyone should stick to the three hundred eight steps instead. Thank goodness we didn't have to work the whole time we were in Ludington during our time off because I really could have gotten myself hurt.

On one of the countless sunny and gorgeous days we had at Pura Vida, I decided to go down the steps to the beach. I really wanted to see our private beach on Lake Michigan. I didn't want to miss out, so I started walking down the long string of steps by myself. Thankfully, there are many landings along the way for sightseeing and rest breaks, so I stopped a couple of times to catch my breath.

As I slowly walked down the steps, I looked at the sandy beach getting closer and closer to me. I couldn't wait to be frolicking on the beach or at least lying down there watching the waves dance along the shore. My paws were ready to feel the cool sand beneath them when Mom unexpectedly grabbed my collar. Where did she come from? I only made it down four flights of steps before Mom caught up to me. I was really bummed that she showed up and ruined my fun adventure.

Apparently, Mom wanted me to turn around because she knew I would not be able to make it up all three hundred eight steps after we were done playing in the water. Well, she was right because I couldn't even make it up the few steps that I originally came down. Actually, I didn't even try to walk up any of the steps. I immediately said, "I need a little help here. These steps require way too much energy." Of course, Mom just heard, "*Mini bark. Mini bark*," because I was already very out of breath by this point. Long story short, Dad rescued me and carried me up all four flights of steps. Dad really is my hero! He was my hero even when I was at my strongest.

Even though I didn't make it to the beach this day in particular, Dad took me to our beach via boat ride later in the week. Luckily, there is a public boat launch close to our house, so we boarded our boat there. Dad took Happy and me for a boat ride through the channel, past the Breakwater Lighthouse, out onto Lake Michigan, and south to our beach at Pura Vida. Dad lifted me out of the boat so I could play on our beach. The sand was just how I imagined . . . soft, cool, beautiful, and perfect. Happy splashed in the water as I gently strolled through the shallow water along the shore letting the sun warm my whole being. I took a couple of short walks and laid in the sand to make sure I was nice and sandy before we went back to the house. This is the only time my paws have touched our beach at Pura Vida thus far, and I hope it won't be the last.

The time spent on designing blueprints, going to multiple meetings with builders and various subcontractors, and supervising as Pura Vida was being built, basically consumed an entire year for our family. This brought our year almost full circle bringing me within five weeks of my fifteenth birthday. Fifteen in canine years supposedly equals anywhere from eighty-eight to one hundred fifteen in human years according to various age conversion tables I've seen in different veterinarians' offices. Pretty impressive, don't you think? I can't believe another year has almost passed since my big fourteenth birthday bash. Unfortunately, I have not made it to fifteen yet, and I'm not sure my health will allow me to have another round of birthday cupcakes hot out of the oven.

Sadly, I've been sick on many occasions over the past year. Each time I don't feel well, Mom and Dad get teary-eyed (Mom more than Dad, as usual). They lie down beside me, pet me, and reminisce about our fun adventures in the past. Certainly, the memories make them smile, but I still see their tears and sadness when I look into their eyes. When I see their unhappiness, I feel I have disappointed them, which is completely opposite of my entire meaning in life. Regrettably, I got *really* under the weather while on our vacation time at Pura Vida in September 2009 while Dad was gone on a kayak trip.

It was another sunny day at Pura Vida, and unfortunately, I felt very exhausted. I thought I was sleepy because I had a big weekend; however, later I figured out I was exhausted for another reason.

Over the previous weekend, we had a houseful of friends and family; we played for three days straight. Everyone, including me, had wonderful meals throughout the weekend. One night I even had carrot hash poured over my lamb and rice hard dog food, and Ethan and I ate every last morsel. Yes, our one year old at home likes to nibble on dog food. Mom tries to make him stop, but he keeps finding it and nibbling on it. He actually races to the closet where our dog food is stashed when Mom opens the door to fill our bowls. Ethan does everything possible his little twenty-one pound frame can manage to get him closer to the gold. It is funny to watch Mom try to keep him out of the food. He is quite strong for being only one year old. Anyway, I don't see what the big deal is because she has let me eat this stuff for years. It must be good for everyone . . . right?

As I've mentioned before, I keep losing weight for no apparent reason, so Mom and Dad give me anything and everything to keep weight on me. As a result, I get lots of "people food" these days. Little did they know that I started a diet pill a year ago so they would start giving me what I wanted. All dogs should get this memo when they are much younger than fourteen so they can enjoy the good life forever and ever. Of course, I am just teasing, but it sounds like a good plan after all, doesn't it? You young pups out there need to be taking notes. By the way, my story is not available in Cliff Notes.

After our visitors left from the busy weekend at Pura Vida, Mom followed the normal bedtime routine. She gave Ethan a quick bath, got him dressed in pajamas, read him a story, and put him in bed. Then she picked out Eddie's pajamas and started his bath. While Eddie was marking all over the garden tub with his new and improved bath crayons, she let me outside to potty. As you know, I used to go exploring at our home in Fruitport whenever I got the chance; Mom and Dad tried gates, bells, and flashers to keep me safe and in our yard. For unknown reasons, I have not wandered far away one time while playing outside at Pura Vida. I have been very good! Therefore, Mom and Dad have gotten really lax when they let me out to do my business. Lately, I have not been wearing a bell or anything. They just let me out on the honor system, which I really enjoy.

Once outside, I started sniffing everything I could, checking the perimeter twice, and looking for unexpected treats. It was a peaceful night with a sky full of twinkling stars.

Without warning, I got really dizzy and nauseous. Simultaneously, my vision became blurry, and my balance was off completely. At this point, I was scared and wanted to wander off so my family would not have to see me like this. I did not want to disappoint them anymore. However, as I tried to wander, I ended up falling over beside the road next to the driveway.

I knew something was really wrong with me since every time I tried to stand up I absolutely could not make it. I decided to simply lie there and let my strength build back up so I could try it again. Eventually, I realized I absolutely could not stand up regardless of how hard I tried. I continued to lie there, filled with worry, in the wet grass and cool night's air. I looked and looked for a shooting star to wish upon but never saw one.

Thankfully, the road in front of our house is not very busy; however, I was still very concerned. What if a car came along and hit me? Would my mom be able to find me out here? What if hungry coyotes found me? There were many unhappy scenarios to consider.

These times are terrible for anyone, especially a dog. If you are a human, maybe you could hit your Lifeline button, crawl to a phone for help, or at least lie on your own floor until someone comes to assist you. I was simply out of luck. I had to stay out on the wet grass beside the road until a stranger stopped to help me or until my mom found me. Unfortunately, my mom was busy giving my three-year-old brother Eddie a bath, so I knew she couldn't be my knight in shining armor. As you can see, my situation did not seem hopeful. I knew my dad would have come to rescue me, but he was kayaking on the Pere Marquette River. The situation was out of my control; this is what was meant to be.

Moments later (much to my surprise), I saw our Suburban's brake lights as Mom was backing down the driveway. I instantly said, "This is my lucky night after all." I saw the Suburban getting closer and closer. The next thing I knew I was centered in the middle of Mom's high beams as she backed out onto the road. Immediately, she came to a stop. I knew the Mommy tears were flowing at this point, but I could not get up and tell her that I was o.k. because I wasn't. I could see Eddie's silhouette in the car with Mom; I felt even worse that he had to see me like this. Mom proceeded to slowly drive the Suburban back up the driveway. I'm sure she was taking Eddie back to the house to let him watch more "kids' shows" as he calls them. "Kids' shows" seem to fix everything for Eddie.

I can't tell you the number of times Mom has come looking for me in our S.U.V. I know when the Suburban fires up late at night that it is time for me to get home and act innocent. However, tonight did not end like all of the other unguided tour nights with my tail between my legs, Mom making me jump up in the S.U.V., and Dad threatening me with sleeping outside for the night.

Instead, Mom walked out with a flashlight and Dad's sweatshirt to see what happened. At this point, she didn't know if I was dead or alive. She was afraid I had been hit by a car and was no longer breathing. On a very happy note, Mom found me alive and breathing with eyes wide open. I even managed a small tail wag upon her discovery of me. Mom hugged me close and just laid with me for a moment or two, relieved to know I was alive and still at home.

Of course, she cried when she found me. I read her lips as she said, with tears flowing freely down her face, "Gunther, don't you dare leave us. We love you and need you. We will get through this." Mom does cry easily, but this time definitely warranted some good tears. She even covered me up with Dad's sweatshirt to make sure I wasn't cold. I felt so exhausted that I couldn't talk back to her. I only wagged my tail again slightly and looked into her eyes so thankful she found me.

Mom said, "Alright, let's get you inside away from this dangerous road." Soft carpet sounded good to me, but unfortunately I was not able to stand. After lots and lots of physical help and encouragement, Mom boosted me up and assisted me with walking back to the garage where I have two super-soft doggy beds stashed. While I was walking, my legs kept crossing at various and random times which made my balance very poor. I was not trying to walk like this. My body just kept doing this. What was going on? I fell over a couple of times even with Mom's help. I felt very weak and uncoordinated. Finally, we made it back to the garage even though it took a ridiculously long time.

Mom debated calling Dad, but she did not want to make him sad while he was away from his family on an adventure. However, she wondered if there was anything she should be doing differently to make me feel better quicker.

After we returned to the garage, Mom went in and immediately got Eddie in bed. A few minutes later, Eddie came out of his room and apparently told Mom that he was not tired. Mom quickly told Eddie that he needed to go to sleep so we could get up early the next morning and go to the beach. She carried him back into his bed and kissed him goodnight. Immediately, Mom locked the front door and brought a video baby monitor, computer, and glass of red wine out to the garage through the garage door.

The comical part of this whole crazy and dark situation was that my mom accidentally locked herself outside the house and had to sleep with me in the garage. Apparently, she didn't realize the lower lock on the door was in the lock position when she closed the door behind her. She quickly discovered this when she could not get the door open as she tried to go inside for a blanket for us. I knew she was already contemplating sleeping with me because I was not feeling very well, but now she had no option.

I was resting/sleeping in the garage because neither one of us had the strength to get me up and down the steps to enter and exit the house. The garage was my only option for the night and apparently Mom's, too. Both of the little ones plus Happy were inside the house snug in their beds. We had no keys stashed, but I bet we would get this fixed first thing in the morning. (Stashing a key should be the first thing on a new homeowner's "to do" list.)

Mom realized she was locked out just a few minutes after she put Eddie in bed the second time, so she immediately ran around to the one tiny open screen in the house and yelled, *"Eddie! Eddie! Eddie!"* She even rang the doorbell multiple times, which caused Happy to bark like a wild woman and dance around the tile floor with her happy paws. Never did little Eddie come down to open the door for us. He must have been sound asleep, dreaming about going to the beach first thing in the morning.

I was excited to have a snuggle buddy. Snuggling with Mom and Dad is one of my favorite pastimes. Mom even slept with me last night on the floor inside the house in Dad's sleeping bag since I can no longer get in the bed beside her. Again, I have to be touching "my people" whenever I get the chance to fully protect them and show them how much I care. I know Mom didn't sleep well all night in the garage because she was worried about me, the kids being locked in the house alone, and spiders crawling on her. Nevertheless, I really appreciated Mom staying beside me throughout the night. I slept most of the night snug as a bug in a rug. I rested peacefully except when my breathing got very rapid and shallow. My breathing has been doing this on and off lately.

Eddie rescued us in the morning when Mom heard him say, "Good Morning, Happy!" on the monitor. I will never forget the hilarious look on Eddie's face when he saw Mom at the front door wanting him to let her into the house first thing in the morning. Luckily, he is a smart kid and was able to let Mom in the door. By this time, I still needed help standing up. Once I got help to stand, however, I could walk short distances on my own and do my outside business as needed. Now Mom and I just needed Dad to get home from his lollygagging on the river so we could take a nice nap *inside!*

Who knows what tomorrow will bring? Regardless, I know I will cherish every last moment I have here on Earth with my family and friends. I pray I can make it to my fifteenth birthday on October 29, 2009, but we will see what the big guy upstairs has in store for me. Hopefully, if I continue to live Pura Vida to the best I can, I will be blessed with at least another birthday, if not many more.

Whether it is God, my parents, Happy, or my "little brothers," I never know what plans are in store for me day to day. Your guess is as good as mine for what each day's events will hold. I am always along for the ride.

Gunther and Princess Happy are always along for the ride.

Along for the Ride

Literally, I have been along for the ride in many vehicles like most doggies. My favorite vehicle to ride in is Dad's old green Chevy pick-up. I enjoy sitting up front with Dad while hanging my head out the window and smelling the fresh air. His truck is always full of supplies for fishing, camping, hunting, and home improvements; sometimes it is hard to find a spot to sit. I don't mind. I just pop a squat on top of duct tape, hunting vests, tackle boxes, or anything else that is in my way. Dad's truck always takes us to exciting destinations, such as a river, various hunting preserves, or the dump. Oh, there are so many intriguing smells at the dump. This is definitely a spot I would like to explore, but I never get the green light to do so. I'm not sure why.

Besides the green pick-up, we have a Suburban that we comfortably travel in frequently. We fill this up easily, as you can imagine, with a family of six, including Mom, Dad, Ethan, Eddie, Happy, and me. However, all of our vehicles have not been comfy with plenty of room to stretch out. For example, Mom used to drive a candy-apple red Saturn with bucket seats back in her college days. Obviously, I don't get to vote when it comes to car shopping, so I just had to keep quiet on this choice.

I've been on many memorable trips in Mom's speedy Saturn. One trip that really stands out to me occurred while we were driving through downtown Indianapolis to get to a bookstore before closing time. As you can guess, we were in a hurry, and Mom had the pedal to the metal. Apparently, cops really do like the color red because an officer immediately turned his lights on as we zoomed by him and followed us until we stopped.

I usually go nuts over men in uniforms, as all doggies do. Possibly it's because they sometimes think they are tougher than I am or they never have dog treats for me. Either way, I was prepared to tell the officer a thing or two until he strolled up to the car and I was face to face with his gun resting nicely in his holster. I decided to lie down uncomfortably in Mom's bucket seats and keep my mouth closed. I remained speechless throughout the whole visit with the police officer and acted more like a mouse than a dog.

Unfortunately, Mom ended up getting a ticket. I felt bad about her ticket, but Mom was speeding and there was nothing I could do to change that fact. Grandpa always tells me, "Your mom has a lead foot." I've come to the conclusion that it is expensive when Mom gets behind the wheel.

After driving off *without* the blue lights following us, Mom said, "Gunther, why didn't you say anything?" I quickly said, "What did you expect? I know to respect a gun in any situation, especially when it is staring me in the face. I'm no dummy!" Certainly, Mom only heard, "*Bark! Bark! Super serious bark!*" but at least I gave her something to think about. It was a quiet ride home afterwards.

I'm sure Mom's blood pressure was sky high after this incident. Luckily, Mom is aware of the research that shows drinking a glass of wine a day helps your heart. I guess Mom wants a really healthy heart. My pheasant hunting days in Fennville, Michigan, helped Mom accomplish this. Many times, Happy, Dad, and I went hunting at Top Gun Pheasant Preserve. Occasionally, Mom accompanied us. She loved watching us dance through the fields looking for birds and taking pictures when we found them. However, she did have an ulterior motive to go pheasant hunting with us . . . wine.

Fenn Valley Winery is just a short distance from our favorite hunting preserve. It was very common for us to hunt, hunt, hunt for hours, then drive to the winery for Mom and Dad to taste wine afterwards. Happy and I never cared because we were exhausted from hunting; we always slept in the truck while Mom and Dad were getting healthy hearts. It was funny to people watch at the winery on the days that we weren't completely exhausted. Every person came out of the winery with a smile on his face. Some people even came out with boxes and boxes of wine in their hands. Too bad Happy and I never went inside. It looked like fun! Maybe Happy and I can be winery dogs one day if Mom and Dad ever get their dream winery open. The life of a winery dog seems like a good life; however, a winery dog must be photogenic because sometimes he ends up on a wine label or in a winery dog calendar.

I'm not sure if I'm photogenic enough for a wine label. Apparently, my mom thinks I am because she takes my picture frequently and has taken me to JC Penney Portrait Studio for family pictures. Going to JC Penney Portrait Studio in the mall was definitely not on my travel radar. As you can see, I never know where my parents will take me next.

Mom decided to have Happy and me in professional family portraits with Baby Eddie in March 2007. He was about nine months old when Mom got this bright (or *not so bright*) idea. Mom discovered that JC Penney's periodically takes family portraits including house pets, so Mom got us on the appointment calendar right away. I was excited to see how these portraits worked. I know there is always a lot of hype building up to family pictures (at least this is true at our house). Mom and Dad are usually extremely stressed out trying to get everyone fed, dressed, and to the appointment on time. The biggest challenge was to get Eddie there on time without him spitting up on his new baby clothes. Mission almost impossible! I was curious to see if this stress was really worth it.

At least Happy and I always have our birthday outfits on for pictures or any other event, so we were pretty low maintenance for pre-picture preparation.

Happy and I jumped in the car when everyone was ready. We rode in the back of the Suburban for a few minutes until we arrived at The Lakes Mall in Muskegon, Michigan. I've been to the mall parking lot many times, waiting on Mom to "just run in" when thirty minutes later she shows up with more than one bag hanging off her arms. I have always wondered what it was like to go in the mall; I finally got to peek for myself.

Mom and Dad buckled Eddie in the stroller and put leashes on Happy and me. It was *go time*! All five of us rushed in a few minutes late for our twelve-twenty appointment. We always try to be on time; it just doesn't happen much. Maybe Mom, Dad, and Eddie should just wear their birthday suits to save lots of time for future appointments. Happy and I do. What would be wrong with this?

There were so many smells and not enough time to enjoy all of them. I smelled every piece of clothing I could see as we walked back to the portrait studio. Dad had to keep tugging on my leash to keep me on track so we would not be later than we already were. On the other hand, Happy stayed close to Dad when walking into and through the mall. She was weirded out by being in this unchartered dog territory. I thought all girls liked to shop. I guess not. Regrettably, we saw no other doggies there for pictures; I was hoping to meet some new canine buddies.

Penney, an actual employee at JC Penney's, took us back for our photo shoot, and the fun was just getting ready to begin. Dad lifted Happy and me onto a table that stood about three feet off the ground. I guess we couldn't be in the pictures unless we were on the table. The funny thing is that all five of us could not fit on the table together at the same time; we actually could not get a full family portrait. Certainly, this defeated the whole purpose, but how were we supposed to know? (I believe the digital age has corrected this situation, so this is no longer a worry.)

Thankfully, at nine months old, Eddie was not walking yet, so he sat still between Happy and me and never tried to get down from the table. Naturally, Mom and Dad were ready to catch Eddie at any minute in case he decided to crawl off the table. We got some fun pictures with our "little brother" Eddie which we will cherish forever. Happy kept jumping down from the table, and Dad kept putting her back up there. Happy definitely did not like the photo shoot; I didn't mind it one bit. I have been in front of a camera all of my life since Mom takes pictures frequently.

Saying, "Cheese," for the camera can be quite time-consuming especially when Christmas card photos are involved. We spend hours and hours every December trying to get the perfect picture for our Christmas card. Our family and friends love these cards, but they don't understand all of the work that occurs behind the scenes.

Before Eddie and Ethan were around, Happy and I were wrapped up as presents, dressed up with reindeer antlers and Christmas kerchiefs, or made to sit on a stuffed Santa's lap for various Christmas cards. Now we get to do some of these same scenes with Eddie and Ethan placed in the picture, too. Talk about a challenge! If it isn't Happy running off, it is Ethan sucking his thumb, or Eddie sticking out his tongue. It definitely takes a while to get the perfect picture. Last year we ended up sending out pictures with Mom in the background in her pajamas. I guess we can't catch everything.

Sadly, Mom and Dad just ordered this year's Christmas cards from a portrait studio because they ran out of time. Therefore, we didn't do our traditional home Christmas photo shoot, and Happy and I were technically cut from the Christmas card for the first time ever. Happy and I missed not being included in the cards this year. Many of our friends and family members noticed and were concerned that we were no longer around. No worries! Happy and I are still here and hope to be included in next year's home photo shoot.

Speaking of Christmas, I think of the times I went shopping for Christmas trees with my family. I loved sniffing the hundreds and hundreds of trees that were waiting to come home with us. They all were great to me, but Mom and Dad always seemed to have trouble finding that perfect one.

Once the selection was finally made, Mom surprisingly took pictures while Dad cut the chosen tree down with a very dull saw. Every year he says, "This blade is so dull. I need to sharpen this thing." The blade continues to be dull as ever. Next Dad dragged the tree towards the Suburban and crammed it into the back with Happy and me in tow. This was the best part because we smelled like pine trees for days, which I know is a much better scent than we normally have. The only drawbacks were the pokey pine needles that stuck in our fur. I can handle pokey pine needles any day to enjoy the smell of a Christmas tree in our house and to see how much the tree makes Eddie and Ethan smile.

I have done other fun things during the holidays beside professional portraits and picking out Christmas trees. I've participated in activities, such as the Jingle Bell Run in downtown Indianapolis, Indiana. Happy and I even got a tiny bell for our collars for the 5 K run. What an experience this was to hear thousands of jingle bells ringing as people and doggies ran in their festive holiday costumes to raise money for the Arthritis Foundation. We even saw Santa Clause in his red suit participating in the race. I never knew Santa could run, especially without his reindeer pulling him along. This charity event was many years ago when I was in tip-top shape, so Mom and Dad actually had trouble keeping up with me.

The only other organized run I did was The Outback Scramble, which was also in Indianapolis. The Outback Scramble is a wacky five mile cross-country run that benefits Gleaner's Food Bank. I even carried two cans of green beans in a bag in my mouth before the run to donate to the hungry. Since this was before Happy's time, I did this along with my buddy Kodi Dog. We had a ball running through the woods for a good cause. I know these early runs inspired me to take multiple unguided tours later in life.

As you can see, Mom and Dad sign us up for many activities to keep us fit as fiddles. One of my favorite activities is water skiing. I have been water skiing with my parents for years. No, that isn't a typo. I guess I actually didn't water ski, but I was just as important as the water skier. I was the observer. Three individuals—the driver, the observer, and the skier—are needed to go water skiing legally.

In the summer of 2000, Dad bought a house on Gun Lake in Shelbyville, Michigan, and Mom bought a boat to accompany the house. I think this was a fair deal. Mom and Dad came home with a 1999 Malibu Sportster LX after boat shopping all over Michigan. I have gotten really good with my boat lingo because boats have been a very large topic of conversation at our house over the years.

Since Dad liked to go water skiing as much as possible, Mom and I were both along for the ride. Dad felt very comfortable skiing since he grew up water skiing on Cordry Lake in southern Indiana. On the contrary, Mom had limited experience water skiing and would rather sit back on the boat and relax in the sunshine. I didn't mind who went skiing; I just wanted someone to keep driving the boat around so my ears could flap in the wind as I enjoyed the beauty of the lake all around me.

The observer's job on a boat is to watch the skier at all times and let the driver know when the skier has fallen down so the driver can come back and pick up the skier safely. I became our observer because it was hard to find a third person to go skiing with us when we had time to go. I've always been a good observer in other capacities, such as watching the door constantly for intruders. No wonder I was the perfect choice for the observer position on the boat. Dad trained me to bark when the skier fell. It took me a couple of tries to get this down, but soon it was a pretty easy job. Of course, I was rewarded heavily with treat after treat when I performed well. Too bad we can't go water skiing in the winter. I miss my extra treats during the cold months.

Everything was perfect with our plan with me as the observer until Mom went and screwed it up. We were skiing on a beautiful evening in the fall. The sun was sinking in the background with purple, pink, and blue streamers lining the sky. (I have brushed up on my colors thanks to my "little brother" Eddie.) Mom was skiing while Dad was driving the boat. Mom decided to let go of the rope at a very bad time; she dropped right in front of a water cop. I started barking right away as I was supposed to do. As you can imagine, the cop didn't fall for my super-cool observer skills, and we got a *big fat ticket*! Have you noticed a theme here with my mom, tickets, and me as an innocent bystander? Ladies will get you into trouble. Watch out for them, fellows.

I don't condone canines as boating observers, and we definitely don't do this anymore. Boating needs to be taken very seriously, and people can be severely hurt if someone does not follow the rules. Please always have a third human as the observer to prevent any accidents. Thanks for being responsible. However, please don't forget to take your doggies with you boating.

Besides running and skiing, I have helped Mom stay in shape many other ways. I can't tell you how many times I have watched and cheered Mom on while she did aerobics, Taebo, Yoga, or Pilates in the living room.

Unfortunately, she has stepped on me by accident many times along the way, but I have always been a good sport since I am along for the ride. She even sticks her feet under me sometimes for leverage so she can have a good abdominal workout. It is fun being Mom's personal trainer.

Naturally, I am not always running or assisting with abdominal training during my adventures with Mom and Dad. They usually take Happy and me with them wherever they go unless they fly on a plane. They refuse to let us fly because they are not sure how we would handle this. I think it would be very cool to fly in a plane as long as I got to sit in a comfy seat with beverages and snacks. However, I don't think it would be cool to be stored with the luggage during a flight. The closest I have ever come to flying is jumping off of our dock to swim. I love this short period of time when I fly through the air with my tail spinning circles like a propeller the entire time. I always wish this time would last longer, just as I wish all of the times would when I am having fun.

Mom took flying lessons in the past, but didn't have time to complete her pilot's license. I know once she resumes and finishes her training in the future that she won't make Happy or me fly beside the luggage; she will let us be her co-pilots. I think all large breed dogs in America need to start an organization called "Freddy Flies First Class" and refuse to fly in the luggage compartment. This is definitely a project I have for my "to do" list.

Even though Happy and I don't travel by plane (yet), my parents are not afraid to take us with them by car for long trips. An obvious destination includes going to see my grandparents in Petersburg, Indiana, which is about an eight hour drive from our house in Michigan. This is definitely a long trip with many challenges, including traveling with my one- and three-year-old "little brothers," but it is well worth the effort.

Grandpa and Grandma have many acres of land for Happy and me to explore. As you can guess, Happy tends to stay close to the house, and I go all over. They also have a lake and a pond where we like to splash, play, and chase the occasional Blue Heron. I enjoy my long walks with Grandpa around the lake. It seems that Grandpa gets stuck with Happy and Gunther duty when we come to visit because Mom, Dad, and Grandma are very busy taking care of Eddie and Ethan.

Luckily, I know Grandpa likes to spend time with us, too. Besides, he has to be on guard when I go outside so I don't escape to neighbor Clifford's house. When I first heard about Clifford living next door, I got very excited, but I soon found out he was not enormously large and red in color. Neighbor Clifford is a Golden Retriever with really big paws. He is still great but doesn't have his own cartoon like the Clifford we all know and love.

At Grandma and Grandpa's, I love cooling my feet off in the lake on hot summer days and following the scent of deer in the fall. In the winter, I enjoy watering Grandpa's outdoor Christmas lights, and in the spring I enjoy watering Grandma's tulips. Never a dull moment at Grandma and Grandpa's!

A trip to my grandparents is a routine trip, but Happy and I have been on some unusual trips, too. Some of the funny places we have visited include multiple hotels across Indiana, Illinois, and Michigan, Cedar Point in Sandusky, Ohio, and casinos in northern Michigan.

I love staying in hotels. We get to watch Animal Planet on the soft bed while Mom and Dad go out to have a night on the town. After dinner, they usually bring us tasty treats, including steak and rolls with lots of butter. Thank God for the invention of the doggy bag.

My favorite hotel stay was on Mackinac Island in Michigan. We took our first ferry ride on the Shepler Ferry Line from the mainland to the island. As always, I tried to mingle while Happy sat as close as she could to Mom's legs the whole ride. At night, Happy and I chilled out in the swanky Mission Point Resort. During the day, we played and ran all over the island and cooled ourselves off periodically in the refreshing waters of Lake Huron surrounding Mackinac island. In between running and playing with Mom and Dad, Happy and I accompanied them to restaurants, such as the French OutPost, and sat in the sunshine enjoying table scraps.

We left Mackinac Island the next day and drove north into Michigan's Upper Peninsula (U.P.). We headed to Munising in the U.P. so Mom and Dad could see the famous Pictured Rocks National Lakeshore. Mom and Dad were told a boat ride was the best way to see the Pictured Rocks; they signed up immediately since we didn't have *Ruffin' It* in tow. Unfortunately, Happy and I weren't allowed on this boat cruise to see the multi-colored rocks with unbelievable shapes. At least we saw postcards and Mom's pictures, so we could pretend we were on the cruise.

Before the boat tour started, Mom and Dad took us hiking on a winding trail that led down to Lake Superior. I am always drawn to any body of water even if it is freezing cold; Happy and I bounced down the trail to splash very briefly in Lake Superior. It was chilly, but it was still fun.

Casinos and Cedar Point were a different story than our hotel stay on Mackinac Island because we didn't actually get to go inside; we only saw the parking lots and the entrances and exits. It was intriguing and entertaining, however, trying to figure out who the high rollers were as they left the casinos at all hours of the night. As you can guess, Happy and I weren't tall enough to go on any rides at Cedar Point, so we had to sit in the car again and wait for Mom and Dad. We had tons of fun listening to people scream for their lives on the Magnum Roller Coaster and watching people walk in and out of the park with smiles plastered on their faces.

After Mom and Dad had their fair share of thrills at Cedar Point, they took us to play in a park by the water to make up for our day in the car. This water happened to be Lake Erie. As you can see, I've been swimming in four of the five Great Lakes: Lake Michigan, Lake Huron, Lake Superior, and Lake Erie. I wonder what my parents' plans are to give me a chance to swim in Lake Ontario. Maybe I should take Mom to see *Phantom of the Opera* on Broadway in New York. Then we could swing by Lake Ontario on the way home for a quick swim.

Just so you don't worry, Mom and Dad always make sure we have plenty of food and water along with suitable weather when we stay in the car for any period of time. They are both huge animal lovers and would never do anything to harm Happy and me.

Actually, Mom is such an animal lover that she took canine physical therapy classes a few years ago. She believes that canine physical therapy clinics will be as common as human physical therapy clinics in a few more years. People put an enormous amount of money, time, and energy into their animals these days, and Mom thinks this trend will continue for years to come. Many "empty nesters" treat animals like their long lost children, which results in many royally treated pets. There are even "pet friendly" vehicles on the market these days with options such as a stowable ramp, electric fan, spill-resistant water bowl, rear car kennel, and dog bone floor mats, along with other puppy friendly features. People are definitely forking out some money for their pets, which is excellent news for me!

Thankfully, Mom practiced on me lots and lots while she was going through this canine therapy training. I never knew I had biceps femoris muscles and obviously didn't know they were really tight. The stretches were not very comfortable, but the massage techniques she used periodically were out of this world! Ever since my "little brothers" arrived,

Mom has not had time to give me a massage. I guess I shouldn't feel too sorry for myself. Mom doesn't have time to give Dad many massages anymore either, and he is her husband. Regardless, Mom wants Dad to start training dogs for hunting so she can do therapy on them after a hard day's work. I think this would be a great combination. I know I would enjoy lying on the massage table after a long day of hunting.

I can't let you think that I just have sissy adventures. I am along for the ride for much more exciting and rigorous activities than having my picture taken at the mall, staying in hotels, and getting my tight muscles stretched. Mom and Dad have taken me ice fishing on Gun Lake, camping in many, many secluded places, snowshoeing in the U.P. of Michigan, and hiking on steep sand dunes.

One of my most memorable and rugged moments was camping on the Pere Marquette River with Happy, Mom, and Dad. Over the years, Dad has visited this river multiple times and has taught me it is the fastest river in Michigan. He has also shown me that the Pere Marquette River is a blue river trout stream surrounded by the natural beauty of the Manistee National Forest.

We had the car loaded with all of our camping supplies and were headed northeast for a couple of hours to Baldwin, Michigan, to camp on the Pere Marquette River. Before we could start camping, we searched for the best spot to set up our tent and make a campfire for the night. We ended up in a location marked "No Camping," which is par for the course for my adventures with Dad . . . not so much with Mom.

Mom and Dad carried our camping supplies as I sniffed and peed all the way through the woods looking for our perfect spot to squat for the night. The spectacular location I chose was on a river bend overlooking the water with a steep bluff for Happy and me to explore. When I ran down to the river, I stuck my head in the water multiple times to look for fish, but I had to do it quickly so the water didn't sweep me downstream. Those were the days when I could kick it into four-wheel-drive Gunther and go anywhere I wanted. No terrain could stop me!

Happy and I chased Frisbees, balls, bones, and whatever else was flying through the air that day. We didn't care; we just played as hard as we could. Our great grandma says, "Play hard today because you just don't know what tomorrow will bring and what the good Lord has in store for you."

After a long evening of playing on the steep bluff and splashing in the water, Happy and I were ready to pass out. We slept by the campfire as Mom and Dad unwound from the busy week. Eventually, Happy and I ended up sleeping beside them in the tent even though I have no idea how I got into the tent. I bet Dad carried me. He has a habit of doing this lately.

Our night there was magical. It reminds me of a time when we had no worries. The morning held fishing, fun, and frolicking for all of us. We hated to leave, but those things called work and responsibility loomed ahead for Mom and Dad. It seems like their responsibilities continue to multiply each and every day. If only I could come up with some way to keep them from working around the clock. I will have to keep thinking about this.

As you can see, I have been lots of places and seen lots of things. I've learned to go along with my family even when we don't leave the house. Therefore, pretending is even in my repertoire. For example, Mom and Dad think their king-size bed is so incredibly comfortable that they wish they could stay in it all the time. I agree completely! We have pretended that we can drive it to the kitchen for all of our meals then drive it back to the bedroom for a small nap. We have talked about taking it to the grocery, the movies, wherever. The drive-able, amazingly comfortable bed has many options in our house. Maybe the car companies need to get working on this one after they get their "pet friendly" vehicles all squared away. Everyone would buy one.

Sometimes, we drive our pretend car-bed to pretend church. Mom is always stressed trying to get out of the house on time with Eddie and Ethan in tow for any event, especially church. She says, "It is rude to be late." I say, "Better late than never!" Many mornings our family does not make it to church for various reasons, so Mom gets bummed out and tries to make up for it. As a result, we play church at home many Sunday mornings. We drive the car-bed to the living room and sit in a circle for church. Happy and I usually need a few reminders to stay in one spot. As you can imagine, Eddie and Ethan need at least one hundred reminders to stay seated and sometimes get bribed with fruit snacks and suckers to remain still during pretend church. We sing songs like "Lord of the Dance" and "Joy to the World." Well, Happy and I try our best to sing these songs, but I'm sure we won't be asked to join the choir any time soon. Then we sit and pray about all of our reasons to be thankful. I am always thankful for pheasants, cheese bread, Milk-Bones, king-size beds, and my family. I have learned lots about Heaven and God through our pretend church; however, I was born knowing more than you think about God and his plan. It is no coincidence that God is dog spelled backwards.

Contrary to popular belief, the car-bed is not part of every fun-filled adventure at our house. No driving was needed on my part for this particular adventure that occurred in August 2005. Mom and Dad decided to take Nana and BooBoo to Alaska for ten days to celebrate their fortieth wedding anniversary and leave Happy and me at home. This is the only time that Camp Love-A-Lot was not available for campers. I decided this was o.k., as long as Camp Love-A-Lot didn't start making a habit out of it.

Mom and Dad did not want us to go to a kennel while they were gone on their merry Alaskan excursion, so they made other arrangements for Princess Happy and me. I got pretty good at folding laundry, picking up the mail, answering the phone, and making macaroni and cheese by day nine. What an adventure to take care of ourselves for ten whole days.

Actually, our fun neighbors The O's took very good care of us while my parents were playing in Alaska. The treats were constantly flowing when The O's were on duty. Some of our other great friends, including a yellow Labrador named Nixie, came up to play and stay with us, too. We sure have wonderful friends! Even with people checking on us frequently throughout the trip, however, Happy and I still got a little lonely and ran out of ways to cause a ruckus.

When Mom and Dad finally walked through the front door after their long vacation, Happy and I were hysterically glad to see them. I felt so much excitement throughout my body that I immediately started doing the Two-Legged Gunther Salsa to Happy. Well, I have definitely done this exciting dance to inanimate objects and other canines in the past but never to my own daughter. *Gross!* Now that I look back on it, I guess I could have done many other things to show my enthusiasm when Mom and Dad came home. Hindsight is 20/20, and apparently I was not thinking clearly at the moment. Sorry, Happy!

I'm along for the ride each and every day, and I wouldn't change a thing. I try to appreciate every situation in which I find myself. This is a good lesson for everyone to learn. Besides, these exciting and random adventures with "my people" are a good way to live out my days, however numbered they may be.

"My People"

Who are "my people?" As you know, I have been with Dad (Eric) since I was a six-month-old pup in April 1995, and Dad met Mom (Crystal) about a year later. Eddie and Ethan came along afterwards to fill our lives with much happiness. We are four humans and two dogs swirled into one family. Over the years, I have become very attached to my human family since I left my canine family so very young. I am devoted to my family unconditionally and protecting them is my number one goal. My body and bark may be worn out, but my love for "my people" is strong as ever!

I am always ready to greet "my people" whenever they come home from work, the dentist, the grocery, and yes, even a funeral. Whatever the situation is, plain and simple, I am always waiting for them at home. What other constant in their lives do they have like this other than God? Certainly, God is with them wherever they roam, and I only have home base covered. However, this is still a huge responsibility. Again, it is no mistake whatsoever that God is dog spelled backwards. Maybe God takes a small break when "my people" come home; he knows I have them protected while they are with me.

You may say, "I have a cat which is always around when I come home." Well, many cats are not interactive or available to listen to your feelings. Or maybe you have a tadpole named Zoomie or a hamster named Bob instead. It is hard to hug a tadpole or a hamster when you really need a hug and feel like you are getting hugged back. Trust me, I have tried. I feel the relationships between humans and dogs are unsurpassed by many other human and pet relationships. Naturally, I am a bit biased towards pooches. I actually think some human and doggy relationships exceed many human to human relationships, but I won't expand on this thought.

As a result, I know absolutely everything about "my people." Mom never washes her face at night. Dad jumps into his pants two feet at a time. Eddie loves to eat edamame and work mazes. Ethan likes to suck his right thumb and guard it with his left hand when he feels scared or tired. Happy poops on the driveway when there is snow on the ground. Eddie and Ethan put raspberries on their fingers to have raspberry fingers instead of eating them. Time Out is on the red couch at our house. Mom hugs me tight at night when she hears scary sounds and Dad is not home. The list goes on and on and on! Mom and Dad's parents and closest friends don't even know some of this information about "my people."

As a pup, I talked a lot trying to keep in touch with my momma, siblings, and friends. (This helps explain excessive puppy barking.) As I got older, I noticed that listening was a much better skill to perfect than speaking. Besides, I eventually realized the people in front of me everyday were the people I really wanted to focus on and protect day in and day out. Sometimes you have to leave others behind so you can nurture the relationships staring you in the face.

Since I am such a good listener, I know "my people's" deepest darkest secrets. I can't count the number of times Mom and Dad have poured their hearts out to me while hugging and petting me the entire time. Little did they know that I would write a book later in life. No worries, Mom and Dad. Your precious secrets are safe with me.

I even know things about Dad that Mom doesn't know and vice versa because they tell me everything. I remember Dad's time during residency when Mom and Happy were still in Indiana and Dad and I were in

Grand Rapids. It was very tough on both Mom and Dad to have this five hour drive between them and super busy schedules to accompany the distance. I always listened to Dad whenever he was frustrated with residency and the distance between Mom and him. I accompanied him to the park so he could get some tension out by throwing the Frisbee for me. I would not have had it any differently. I inspired Dad to keep going and get through that tough year. Even though I was frequently alone for twenty-four to thirty-six hours at a time, I would do it over and over again for him. I was always very happy to see him when he got home. We ordered Domino's Pizza at least twice a week, and I loved to share these late-night treats with him. I actually miss those times of sharing pizza into the wee hours of the night.

Likewise, Happy helped to keep Mom and Dad's relationship strong. She listened to Mom every time she was sad or lonely because she missed us. Happy also inspired Mom to keep in shape by running with her through the neighborhood after work and kept her smiling regardless of the situation. Most importantly, Happy kept Mom company and safe on many long and late car rides from Indiana to Michigan after lengthy work weeks.

Unfortunately, one time Happy did not accompany Mom on her long trip from Indiana to see us. There is no need to be worried though because I was there to protect her. When Mom pulled into our driveway at midnight, she noticed a man walking down the street. The next thing she knew, the man stopped right behind her car and did not move. Immediately, she called us. Naturally, Dad sent me out to check on her. I sprinted out the door, barking with my *really deep* and *scary bark*. The random man took off screaming and running as fast as he could. I chased him for at least three blocks. I have never seen anyone run so fast! I think the Olympics could be in his future.

Finally, Dad caught up to us before I had this stranger's loins for a late-night snack. Dad asked, "What are you doing, Mister?" The mystery man replied with breath reeking of alcohol, "I wasn't doing nothing, man! I just needed a ride home." Dad ended their conversation by quickly replying, "If you choose to come back, the big black dog will be the least of your worries!" Neither one of us believed the mystery man's story for a second. Regardless, we protected Mom from this creep, and we never saw him again. I'm not sure what intentions this stranger had. However, Dad and I knew they weren't good, and we weren't shy to tell him about it. As you can see, I happen to be an excellent judge of character and put the safety of "my people" first. Remember, I work for God and have been trained by the best!

Life was much better once Mom and Dad were actually in the same town again. We have shared many amazing times together, such as the first time Mom found out she was pregnant. All of us were so excited! Mom and I sat for hours and hours on my chair (yes, I have my own chaise lounge), in the living room, reading books about breast-feeding, baby sleep schedules, prenatal vitamins, strollers, car seats, etc. I learned so much about babies in this time period that I think I could raise one all by myself now.

This, of course, led to the day when Mom and Dad went to the hospital. At this point, Mom looked like she had eaten one too many double cheeseburgers, but I never told her this. There was just more of her to cuddle with throughout the day. Mom didn't come home with Dad from the hospital the next day, so I was worried. Dad brought Happy and me a tiny blanket with new and exciting smells. Happy and I laid on it, cuddled with it, and slept on it. Dad said, "Happy and Gunther, we have a new member of our family. His name is Eddie, and Mom is still at the hospital with him. We will come home with him tomorrow, so rest up and get ready to be a big sister and a big brother." Happy and I were so excited that we didn't sleep all night because we couldn't wait to meet our little Eddie.

Sure enough the next day came, and Mom and Dad walked in holding this little peanut of a person. They showed him to us immediately. Happy licked his feet while I jumped up, grabbed his tiny yellow hat, and ran off with it. Dad forcefully said, "Gunther, bring his hat back right now!" Instead, I stopped and flipped on my back with my feet in the air. I scratched my back on the ground and wiggled my legs all around. I just needed a belly rub to know that the four-legged family members weren't going to be left out. Dad came over right away and gave me the best ear and belly rub ever.

Since that exact moment, Happy and I knew that we were still important to Mom and Dad, too. I released Baby Eddie's hat right away and went back over to sniff his tiny features. Happy and I both looked forward to playing with Eddie and getting to know him. As Happy and I saw how amazingly happy that Baby Eddie made Mom and Dad, we never had any jealousy towards him. Besides, there is no time for jealousy in this short-lived life.

We obviously had the same emotions when Mom found out she was pregnant again. However, with this pregnancy, she felt very tired and a little nauseous, so Mom and I did not get any reading done. At least, I knew I could coach her through it even though we didn't have time to brush up this time around.

Baby Ethan arrived in April 2008. We were all very excited to meet him! Eddie was a twenty-two-and-a-half-month-old toddler when his little brother arrived. We were all anxious to see how Eddie would act towards his new baby brother. Fortunately, Eddie took to Ethan like he had known him all of his life and has been a wonderful big brother ever since.

Dad also brought us one of Ethan's baby blankets before he came home so we could meet him, too. Instead of being up all night with anticipation this time, Happy and I went right to sleep. We learned after Eddie was born that a good night's sleep was rare with a newborn in the house. Happy and I rested up so we could be on duty when Ethan came home. Once little Ethan was home, Happy and I took turns going out to the living room with Mom to lie beside her in the middle of the night while she nursed Baby Ethan. It was the least we could do to help.

Mom and Dad have recently been talking about having a third baby. Of course, they wonder if it will be a boy since they have three sons (including me), five nephews, and Happy as the only daughter. Happy will work for a few more years, but one day she will have to leave them, too. Maybe I will be reincarnated as their next son because you know if Mom and Dad try again they will have a little boy. However, we'll see what God's plans are for "my people." Boys are obviously wonderful; Mom and Dad would welcome a third boy with open arms.

Happy and I are there for "our people" during these very joyous times. We are also there for "our people" during those times when words can't comfort and tears flow freely. We have been there for hours of hugging and listening when we have found out the loss of loved ones. We have been there every difficult step of the way: when Mom and Dad get the upsetting phone calls; when the initial tears start flowing; when they get ready in their dressy black outfits; when Mom gets stressed out because they are going to be late; when Dad frantically searches for a lint brush to brush our dog hair off their attire (don't they know this is how we comfort them on the run?); and when they have trouble falling asleep that night following the day's heartbreaking events.

Happy and I have shared other not-so-happy times also with "our people," such as when Mom and Dad were in a serious car accident on vacation in the Florida Keys. This car accident remains my scariest moment. Thankfully, God and many guardian angels were watching over them that day.

Happy and I were very glad when we finally saw Mom and Dad come home after their accident. I will never forget how tightly Mom and Dad hugged us as tears trickled down their faces. Happy and I do not know what we would have done if they wouldn't have come home. We nursed them back to health with a lot of help from our entire family and many of our close friends. I know Mom and Dad try extra hard to make every day count now, since February 10, 2001, could have easily been their last.

Likewise, "our people" have been here for Happy and me through all of the ups and downs in our lives. Doggies have sad and disappointing days, too. It has been a tough time over the last two years for some of the furry members in our family. Grandma and Grandpa's miniature Schnauzer Tinky passed away, and we all miss her lively spirit. Even though she was only nineteen pounds, she played with Happy and me like she was also eighty-eight pounds of fur. One of my black Labrador children, Poppy, passed away at the young age of nine. She had cancer and ended up losing her battle after fighting for a few very hard months. I know we all miss her shiny, happy self, especially her "little brothers" Teddy, Crosby, and Nate. The most recent doggy loss we had was my girlfriend Scout. Thankfully, Scout and I spent this last Thanksgiving with our families and went pheasant hunting together. However, we were both so weak we just got to walk around the field for a few minutes. Then we sat in the truck and reminisced about our great memories together.

Cuddling with Mom and Dad and playing with our "little brothers" helped Happy and me through these tough times of losing these furry ones who mean so much to us. I know Tinky, Poppy, and Scout are all watching over us from Heaven, and I will definitely find them when I enter the magical world above.

As you can see, "our people" share many emotions with us, and likewise, Happy and I share many feelings with "our people." We get each other through many emotional moments whether happy or sad. When "our people" share their experiences with us, we want to be there to help them any way we can. Sometimes being a furry shoulder to cry on, a soft belly to rub, or a giant teddy bear for hugging is the best way we can help them in difficult times. Happy and I share the great triumphs and losses of life with "our people," and we can't think of a better way to spend our days.

Luckily, every day is a new day, and I don't always have to be a shoulder to cry on. Long ago I decided to use my God-given traits to the best of my ability to help "my people" in *any* way I can.

This is How I Roll

Have you ever thought about walking around your house on all fours? Well, if you did, you would see the world from a totally different perspective and see how I roll.

I have embraced the fact that I am a dog with four strong legs and a tail, and I am on a different level than grown-ups. Maybe this is why I get along with kids so well because we see the world from a very similar viewpoint: the Gluteus Maximus. (This is another name for a large muscle in your butt. Sorry, I've learned a bit of medical terminology throughout the years helping Mom and Dad study for tests.) I wonder if this is why dogs and kids have such a good sense of humor.

Everything I do on a daily basis is to please or help my family. I lend a paw around the house whenever I can to save them time, money, and energy even though my thoughts of being helpful may be different than theirs. The kitchen is the main area in the house where I feel the most useful.

I love to help out in the kitchen any way I possibly can. Naturally, my favorite kitchen time is when Dad or BooBoo is carving the turkey on Thanksgiving Day. I enjoy being the taste tester to make sure the turkey is safe for my family to eat. Of course, everyday is not Thanksgiving at our house even though it should be because we have so many reasons to be thankful.

I enjoy every minute in the kitchen, as you can imagine. My keen sense of smell makes me crazy for the tasty food that Mom cooks like chicken and dumplings, homemade vegetable soup, and apple pie. I have always wanted to be Mom and Dad's private chef, but I am afraid I will be like Cookie Monster and eat all of the food before I get it to the table. This is the main reason I haven't pursued this chore around the house.

I tend to focus on the after-meal activities every day of the week. I wish Mom and Dad would just relax and let me clear and wash the dishes after meals, but they simply don't. Instead, Happy and I grab any morsels that fly from the highchair or fall from the table thanks to our messy "little brothers." Then we wait for the dishwasher contents to be unveiled. I am embarrassed to admit that I have not yet figured out how to open the dishwasher door. This is most likely due to my lack of opposable thumbs. At least, I am a master at the fridge door. Luckily, our "little brother" Ethan opens the dishwasher frequently, so we have lots of access these days. I giggle when Ethan climbs into the dishwasher to play. Unfortunately, Mom and Dad don't think this is very funny most of the time.

I see licking each and every dirty dish in the dishwasher as my way of saving Mom and Dad time and money. It is only fair because it is at my height, plus it has tasty treats that would go to waste without my intervention. Sometimes I take silverware into the living room for the Super Gunther Wash Cycle. This strong cycle is usually needed for silverware with dried-up spinach casserole or cheesecake on it. Mom cracks up when she finds a fork in the living room the next day. If Mom and Dad would let Happy and me lick all of the dishes clean, they could just put them back in the cabinets so they would be ready for the next meal. They don't see eye to eye with me on this, but I am still working on them. I wonder if a power point presentation will be more convincing. In the meantime, Happy and I will continue to lick all the dirty dishes and silverware we can find.

Once Ethan is out of the high chair, Happy and I go to work! I really enjoy food as you can tell. Even though I feel under the weather sometimes, I still have kept my monstrous appetite. We clean out every tiny cracker crumb or sliver of string cheese we can find in Ethan's highchair or underneath it on the floor. On bonus days, we even find food stuck to the cabinets where Ethan must have thrown some treats that he didn't want to eat. He is very generous to share his edible goodies with us in many ways. However, he needs to stop sharing with us so much because Ethan is only in the eighth percentile for weight. I definitely need to teach this baby boy how to eat. Since Ethan is always very interested in our Milk-Bones and dry dog food, I share with him frequently to help the little guy gain more weight. I think Mom and Dad need to order him pizzas every day to get extra meat on his bones. Of course, I would be willing to help Ethan with the pizzas if he wanted my assistance.

Dinner leads to someone taking out the trash: Mom in the summer and Dad in the winter. I think Mom would prefer to stay in the house for six months during the winter to avoid the cold temperatures, so Dad takes the trash out mostly in the cold weather. Eating the trash is my most effective way to be green, but my parents still don't agree with me on this either. Why put all of this food into the landfills when it could be going into my tummy? I still don't understand why knocking over the trash and self-serving is a problem. I'm just trying to save everyone some time and make sure that Eddie and Ethan's children have a safe place to play and grow up one day.

My kitchen duties extend into the laundry room since spills usually occur in the kitchen and the dirty clothes end up in the washing machine. I lick the kids' clothes with chocolate milk spills, Dad's shirts with buffalo wing sauce, and Mom's pants with peanut butter and jelly on them. Also, I snatch cloth napkins off the chairs on the very few occasions that these are used at our house. I feel it is my job to lick the dirty clothes as clean as possible. Why doesn't Mom just put the clothes back in the closet once I lick them clean? I don't know. She has me puzzled on this one. Hasn't she heard that a dog's mouth is cleaner than hers? Well, I think this is actually a myth because canines lick private areas from time to time, but maybe Mom hasn't thought this through yet. Besides cleaning clothes, I also like to sleep on them, warm them up, and transfer my hair and smell to their contents. This way "my people" won't forget about me during the day while they are out. I am very helpful when it comes to laundry. At least, I think I am.

My responsibilities are much greater than just the kitchen and laundry room. Protecting my family is an endless responsibility. Nose prints on the glass doors are a must as a dog! This tells others to stay away because there is a big black dog that will *eat* them if they mess with anyone in this house. My other attempts to protect "my people" include sleeping by the door while "my people" are away, sleeping in bed with Mom and Dad when my body allows, checking perimeters while doing business outside, always watching the front door, and barking, barking, barking when a stranger is at our door.

Naturally, one of my favorite responsibilities is to protect my "little brothers" while they are fast asleep. I sneak out of my room every night and wander into their room where smiling fish decorate the walls. I stare at Eddie and Ethan's tiny features and wonder what dreams are swirling around in their heads. I am always happy to know they are safe and sound and constantly wish I could tuck them in at night forever and ever.

Actually, my entire being is made to take care of "my people" and make them happy. My *teeth* are for eating anyone who tries to hurt "my people" and of course, for chomping every Milk-Bone in sight. My *nose* is for putting nose prints on the door, sniffing out danger, and finding pheasants. My *four legs* are for following "my people's" every footstep. My *mysterious brown eyes* are for constantly watching over "my people." My *large boxy head* is for opening any door to find "my people" wherever they may be and to have lots of room for dreams about them. My *ears* are now for great ear rubs. Of course, my ears were originally made to hear "my people's" voices, but sadly we know I can't do that anymore. My *old collar* is for "my people" to have long after I am gone. It holds many memories and has lots of character. (Mom, I definitely don't want a new one even though mine is severely ripped. Thanks for sticking it out with her on this one, Dad.) My *large furry body* is for Mom to have someone to cuddle with at night when Dad is working a random late shift. My *big paws* are for holding "my people's" hands when they need me. My *powerful tail* is for showing "my people" how incredibly happy I always am to see them! My *happy heart* is for loving "my people" unconditionally.

This wild world keeps spinning and time doesn't slow down for anyone. I can't believe how quickly my life is passing me by. I've decided to make the most out of everyday and use my God-given traits as best I can to help those close to me. We are here for a reason and all of us need to remember this. Each day has a purpose, and we simply need to find it and live it. Live day to day, stop trying to figure out the past and worrying about the future, and be considerate any way you can. This is how I roll. Thankfully, I've continued to keep rolling on and on and have come to a special day that calls for much celebration, champagne, and cupcakes.

Gunther and his stuffed animal pheasant

Swanky Bubbles

"**Happy Birthday** to Me, Happy Birthday to Me, Happy Birthday Dear Me, Happy Birthday to Me . . . and many more!**" No, I'm not having déjà vu. Today is October 29, 2009, and I am fifteen years old. I can't tell you how happy that I am here today. My parents are overjoyed that I am with them to enjoy another fun birthday party with all the works. I know that I am not as young as I used to be, but I like to think I have gained a lot of wisdom while growing older.

A little bit of knowledge I've learned over the years is to have passion and believe in yourself. Be passionate about anything and everything you do, whether it is brushing your teeth or saving the Earth from utter and complete destruction. Embrace your life goals and go after them. No one else will go after your dreams for you, so you have to give them your all. Regardless of what you believe, believe it to the fullest and do your best *always!* No one can ever ask for more. I was passionate about having a fifteenth birthday and truly believed I would make it to my big number fifteen. Look where the power of positive thinking got me today.

My fifteenth birthday started with stretching on the floor beside the king-size bed where I used to frequently sleep. Maybe I can encourage Mom and Dad to boost me up there for a small nap later today. I slept late this morning which felt great. Dad got up early with my "little brothers" and played with them upstairs so they would not wake up Mom and me. Dad wanted us to sleep late today. He is so thoughtful.

After my third attempt, I stood up and slowly wandered to the door. Dad immediately let me out and gently assisted me down the two steps that lead outside into the wide, wide world. I slowly stretched, breathed in some fresh air, and watered Mom's flowers as I have done many times in the past—just not with as much grace this time. Thankfully, there were no squirrels, rabbits, or cats to greet because I can't chase them anymore. I definitely don't want them thinking they have the upper paw on me.

Once my business was complete, I pushed myself extra hard, made it up the steps, and waited with my big black nose pressed up against the front glass door. Dad saw me and said, "Happy Birthday," as he let me in the house. I was also greeted by three-year-old Eddie who had a birthday hat on his head and a huge smile on his face just for me. Our eighteen-month-old Ethan walked over to me as I was resting on the floor and gave me a huge hug, multiple pats on the head, and a kiss on the cheek. He is such a lover! I see a lot of me in him. Then, as usual, Mom appeared around the corner with birthday hat in place and two cameras in her hands. Dad got me to pose with my party hat on my head so Mom could take lots and lots of pictures of me as the birthday boy. I smiled and smiled and smiled just thinking the whole time how happy I was to be blessed with another year with my amazing family and friends. Secretly, I was thinking about presents and cupcakes, too.

Dad made pancakes from scratch which I enjoyed sprinkled into my regular dog food for breakfast. After I devoured these tasty treats, I knew it was time for my favorite part of my birthday party: cupcakes! Mom made white Funfetti cupcakes the night before so they would be all ready for the celebration. Dad set a cupcake down in front of Happy and me. We posed for pictures with drool hanging out of our mouths while everyone sang "Happy Birthday" to me. Then we ate the cupcakes in less than two seconds. The cupcakes magically disappeared.

It is only breakfast time now, so I look forward to many more cupcakes today and, of course, on my next birthdays. Are there cupcakes in Heaven? I'm just curious. I bet Mom will ship some to me there if God is not a baker. Hopefully, she will not have to do any shipping any time soon because I want to be right beside "my people" for many more years.

Food always makes me feel sleepy, so I decided to take a nap. I needed to rest up because Dad was taking Happy and me pheasant hunting. Dad was worried that I would not be able to do much hunting. I didn't know what I would be able to do either, but I didn't want to worry about it. I just wanted to go for it! A little is better than nothing at all. Whether or not I made it one minute or one hour hunting did not matter to me. I just wanted to spend time with Dad looking for birds in a field. Hunting with Dad makes my whole year!

After my nap, the whole family loaded up in our Suburban and drove to find Gleason Farms in Scottville, Michigan. I slept a little on the way, unlike in the past, when I used to stand up the entire truck ride waiting for the very second to jump out and start my hunting adventures. Once we arrived, I stood up immediately, anticipating what our day held for us in the fields. Happy and I have been to many pheasant preserves over the years, but this was the first time we had been to Gleason Farms. Some of the fields we hunted in the past had high uncut brush that we had to charge through to sniff out the birds. As a result, Happy and I ended up with multiple battle scars, which Mom strongly disliked. Luckily, Gleason Farms looked like it had nice clear paths which would make it much easier for me to maneuver in my golden years.

It is always fun and interesting to explore new territory. Besides, what's not to love about tall grass swaying in the light wind, sunshine peeking through the clouds, fifty-five degree temperature, small puddles periodically to cool my paws, one-on-one time with Dad, and the overall feeling of being one with nature. Doesn't everyone (except pheasants, of course) want to go pheasant hunting?

While Dad went to meet Mr. Gleason, my mind wandered back to all of our past hunting trips. The night before our hunting trips, Dad always laid out his shotgun shells, whistles, boots, and orange hunting vest in the living room. I pranced around the room sniffing every thread and wagging my tail like I'd won the lottery each and every time. I knew he would take me with him, and I couldn't resist the smell of the birds on his hunting clothes. (I still can't.) I slept each night on top of his hunting goodies and dreamed of chasing birds. I was always the first one to jump into the truck the next morning, and I was on high alert the whole way to the pheasant farm because I didn't want to miss a thing.

Once in the field, I immediately put my nose in the air and took off as if I was in a shopping spree at Petco. With time, I learned to point when I found a bird in the field. When pointing, I freeze up once I find a bird to give Dad extra time to catch up with me so he will have a better shot. Pointing takes much self-discipline because I want nothing more than to catch the bird and parade around with him in my mouth to make my dad proud. Instead, I have to take a stiff stance and drool over the bird standing right in front of me until Dad yells, "Release!" I have never had any official hunting classes, but Dad thinks I am a great hunting dog. Everything I know about hunting I have learned from him, so he must be a good trainer after all.

Unfortunately, my breathing got extremely heavy while daydreaming and waiting in the Suburban for Dad to return. Of course, this was due to my excitement about finding birds and my laryngeal paralysis getting worse and worse. It was my birthday though, so let's not think about this latter reason. We waited anxiously as Dad spoke with Mr. Gleason and gave him money for my birthday pheasants. Finally, Dad came back and gently lowered me out of the Suburban while Happy bounced out. I used to bounce out, but my body won't let me do that anymore. Mom asked Happy to get back in the Suburban so Dad and I could hunt alone. I obviously can't keep up with Happy anymore, and Dad didn't want her to chase all of our birds away on my special day.

At once, my nose went straight to the ground and led me through a small section of field searching for that all so familiar scent of pheasants. Again my heart and mind still think I am two years old, but my body keeps telling me I am much, much older. I really wanted to chase birds all over the field and hunt for hours like the old days. Instead, I wandered over a small section of the field and smelled for pheasants with all that I had. I fell down a couple of times due to the uneven ground and my extremely weak hips. However, Dad helped me back up each time, and I kept searching frantically for my birthday presents. Dad closely followed behind me as happy as a lark because hunting with me has always been one of his favorite things to do. I hope he realizes that hunting with him is one of my most favorite things to do also. These times are priceless to me!

To my surprise, I found a bird within a few minutes of being in the field. (Later, I found out that Dad had Mr. Gleason stash some birds in close proximity of where we started hunting so I would have more of a chance at finding a bird on my birthday. Thanks, Dad and Mr. Gleason!) At once, I locked up and pointed at the bird as I have done so many times in the past. This felt absolutely amazing! I think I waited about five seconds until I saw Dad yell, "Release!" At once, I lurched forward to scare the bird. Up, up, up the pheasant flew into the partially cloudy sky and in no time down, down, down he fell. Dad and I went together to find the bird, and we found him lying in the tall brush. I grabbed him and wagged my tail like I was trying to take flight. Dad's smile was as big as it was the first day he met me. I love this look on his face: utter happiness. This is definitely the purpose for my life here on Earth today.

Mom, Happy, Eddie, and Ethan waited patiently in the car while we were hunting. Mom went with us in the past, but my "little brothers" are too young to go hunting; she stayed in the car with them to keep them safe and entertained. After I found my birthday pheasant, she ran over to snap many birthday pictures. I tried to smile as best as I could with a huge bird in my jaws and its feathers tickling the roof of my mouth. I have always said that you can smile with your eyes, and I have gotten very good at this throughout my hunting years.

Unfortunately, during all of this excitement, my breathing got out of control. I ended up teetering over in the field and was unable to get up. Dad ran over to check on me. All of a sudden, I was very concerned because I could not catch my breath regardless of how hard I tried. The expression on Dad's face was not good. I continued to gasp for air and just felt like my breathing and entire life were spinning out of control. As I stared into Dad's eyes, he continued to pet me with a scared look on his face and tears in his eyes while saying, "You're o.k., Gunther. You're o.k., Gunther. You're o.k., Gunther." Thankfully, after a few minutes my breathing began to stabilize, and I started to relax and breathe regularly. I am very bummed that my body responded like this to hunting for just a short time. However, I would not have traded these few minutes for anything else in the world! I need to be thankful for what I am still able to do.

I snoozed all the way home. When we got home, Dad gently lifted me out of the Suburban. I whizzed on Mom's orange daylilies and slowly walked inside and passed out because I was exhausted. At least this part was no different than my past performances. I always hunted so hard that I slept for many hours, sometimes days, once we returned home from our hunting adventures.

Mom, Dad, Eddie, and Ethan left for dinner next, so I slept while they were gone. When they returned home, I was ready to rock and was curious to see what was for my birthday dinner. I got to eat chicken strips and french fries mixed with my dry dog food on my big day. Happy and I ate a cupcake after dinner and crawled in front of the fireplace in the living room. I cuddled right up to Eddie and Dad while Dad was trying to convince Eddie that he was really tired and needed to go to sleep soon. I watched as Eddie and Ethan reluctantly went to bed, as Happy very willingly went to sleep in Mom and Dad's room, and as Mom and Dad cleaned the house. I thanked God then and there for every single moment that he has given me with my family whether it is extraordinary or mundane.

Oh no! I just realized that my wrapped presents were missing from my big celebration. As if on cue, Mom came in from cleaning the kitchen and said, "No worries, birthday boy. I did not forget about your birthday presents. I think you are too tired to really enjoy them tonight, so you can open your presents tomorrow." I think she was right. Besides, now I could dream about my birthday goodies all night long.

After the kids were in bed, I woke up again to see Mom and Dad on the couch in front of the TV and fireplace. The couch ranks second to my king-size bed and is a beloved spot to spend time with Mom and Dad. I laid my head on the couch as I have done for years and years asking permission to get on the couch. In this world, I have learned that good manners get you very far, such as onto a black leather couch. I stared at Mom and Dad with the best puppy dog eyes I could give them and guess what happened? Dad got up and lifted me up to cuddle on their laps. I fell asleep nuzzled between two people who mean more than the world to me. If only I could tell them that. I guess I just did.

At the end of every day, Mom and Dad ask Eddie what his favorite part of the day was and it is so funny to hear what he says. Sometimes Eddie says, "Playing with you Daddy and Mommy; playing with Ethan. Eating pudding. Playing in my sandbox. Going skiing, and eating cookies." Tonight Eddie said, "Singing 'Happy Birthday' to Gunther was my favorite part of today!" How fun is he?

My family usually does not ask me my favorite part of the day because they think I can't hear them anymore. Thankfully, I am still really good at reading lips. I say, "Mom and Dad, my favorite part of every day is simply spending time with you, whether it be while you quickly pet my head as you run out the door or cuddle with you on the couch during a movie. Any acknowledgment from you makes my day! Thank you for making hunting with Dad and eating cupcakes with "my people" my favorite parts of my fifteenth birthday. I know time gets away from us all. I thank you so much for remembering my big day and making it very special. I love you more than you will ever know!"

Turning fifteen makes me so happy that I could dance.

"Dance of Life"

You may enjoy Hip Hop, Folk, Ballroom, Latin, Swing, or Belly Dance, but I greatly enjoy the "dance of life." Of course, with four feet, I always step on my partner's toes, so I really have no other choice.

The "dance of life" requires many important pieces other than just knowing the right steps, having the shiniest coat, wearing comfortable shoes, and having the prettiest or most handsome partner beside you. It requires balance and love as well as giving, sharing, having good manners, and counting your blessings every day.

I try to count my blessings each and every day, but it is easy to get wrapped up in the busy, every day hustle and bustle of checking the perimeter outside, eating Milk-Bones, sleeping in the sunshine, and dreaming about "my people." Even though each day is full of activity, I do my best to remember to count my blessings. I hope everyone does this.

Having good manners gets you very far in this fast-paced modern world. I definitely know the power of the "please" and "thank you." If you don't know this yet, please try it. I think everyone is equal in this world regardless of race, economic position, number of legs, and presence of a tail or lack thereof. (I thought all of my canine buddies would appreciate these last two details.) Practice saying "please" and "thank you" to absolutely everyone more often, and unexpected doors will open for you on your journey through life.

Since my parents have taught me good manners, I know thank you letters are a must when someone does something nice for me. I want to write one now so "my people" know how much they mean to me just in case they haven't been paying attention.

Thank You! Thank You! Thank You:

God and my guardian angels for every single day I have with my family and friends.

Mom and Dad for the never-ending adventures and for being *you*.

Happy for being my little princess and constant partner in crime.

Eddie and Ethan for sharing your tiny hugs, sweet kisses, and constant smiles.

Grandma and Grandpa for sharing your couch with me and giving me lots of table scraps when Mom and Dad weren't looking.

Nana and BooBoo for putting up with "Gunther Follies" and always leaving a light on for me at Camp Love-A-Lot.

Scooter for wanting me to play Frisbee with you so I would eventually meet Eric and be the happiest pup alive.

Memphis for spending time with me and giving us our beautiful babies.

My list could go on and on; I have met many wonderful people in my lifetime. Thank you also to absolutely anyone who has ever caused me to smile because helping someone smile is priceless and goes much further than you can ever imagine!

Saying "please" and "thank you" will help keep your "dance of life" off the toes of those close to you. Fortunately, giving and sharing all you can will also be beneficial to keeping the balance you need in everyday life.

Give in any way you can, and you will soon find out why it is better to give than to receive; there are many ways to give. Giving and sharing go hand in hand with keeping the "dance of life" in check. Just pay attention to detail and you will quickly learn who is in need. Even though you may have piles of treats, a toy box full of squeaky animals, and endless dog food, it doesn't mean the German Shepherd down the street does also. Whatever the situation, be aware, and lend a paw when you can.

If you can donate money to your favorite charity, such as Leader Dogs for the Blind or Guiding Eyes for the Blind, then go for it. In case you aren't familiar with these charities, they support training canines to assist the blind in their daily lives and give them more independence. I respect all of the pooches who train for this huge responsibility. Naturally, Mom and Dad take care of my contributions currently, but at least I suggest great places to put their assistance. I still need to think of a way to make my own offerings one day.

However, if you do not have any extra money laying around, then be creative. Maybe someone could use the knowledge you learned in school to make his or her day easier and more productive. Possibly a stray dog is hungry and needs somewhere to call home. Maybe a young couple in the neighborhood with small children could use your free time for a date night that they could not afford otherwise. Whether you volunteer at an animal sanctuary, give your favorite dog many, many ear rubs, visit the elderly in a nursing home, or sell Christmas trees at your church, please remember that giving your time is a very powerful present.

As you are spreading good will, please remember The Golden Rule: Do unto others as you would have them do unto you. (I really did listen during play church at home.) Think about it. It makes a lot of sense and will make for a much nicer life for you if you follow this rule religiously.

Good will, of course, makes me think of "playing the Goodwill Game" as Mom likes to call it. When Mom mentions this game, I know it is time to clean out my toy box and share. I think it is a great idea to donate any items that no longer get any use. For example, why let someone go without any warm clothes while many of your winter clothes sit in the closet to keep only the shelves warm? I would love to donate some of my gently used clothes, but I can't seem to get them off of me. At least, I never have to worry about losing a hat, scarf, or sweater.

It is never too late to bring a positive light into the world however you decide to do it. I truly believe any good deed goes a long way. Hopefully, your good deeds will come full circle one day inspiring those around you to help, help, help!

Love will ultimately keep the balance in your daily life. Whether it be your wife, husband, amazing and adorable black Labrador Retriever, grandparent, or good friend, love every one of them because each day is unknown for all of us. If you truly love those you deeply care for, then you will dance your way through all of your days, including the most difficult ones, instead of just making it through them.

Even though my physical balance is off many days, my "dance of life" has never been better. I plan to continue Fox Trotting my way through this world as long as I can. Always let the inner you shine through and remember to dance. Don't step on any feet, just be *very* near.

If I Can't Be At Your Feet

In *my eyes*, I have become very wise throughout my fifteen years here on Earth. I feel I have learned so much, but I wish I had another fifteen years because I still have a lot to experience. Never stop learning! You can never know everything about a situation no matter how much of an expert you are. Unless, of course, you are God, then this paragraph does not apply to you.

I've discovered that some people have a longer time than others to make their impression in this world. I constantly wonder why my time here is relatively longer than many other four-legged friends. I know God has his plan for all of us, and I believe he still needs me here to protect and help my family. I thank God each day for every moment I have with "my people."

I have many secrets for a long and happy life: frequent naps; dogged desire for exploration; many Milk-Bones; countless hours of Frisbee, hunting, and swimming; a king-size bed; a positive attitude in every situation; and thinking outside the doghouse. Luckily, I was always an inside dog so I never had trouble with this one.

Fine pieces of modern technology may have been helpful also in prolonging my happy life. My elevated dog bowl helped to prevent me from getting Wobbler's Syndrome (something else Mom learned about in her canine therapy classes). My doggy ramp made it easy on my joints to get in and out of *Ruffin' It* on our hundreds of water trips. Arthritis medicine has helped me stand up even on really painful days. My doggy seatbelt has protected me with Mom's crazy driving. My festive holiday outfits kept me smiling during the holiday hustle and bustle. In addition, my multiple adventures and travels have kept my spirit forever young.

However, Mom and Dad, my biggest secret to longevity is *being at your feet*. I show you my unconditional love by being as close to you as possible day in and day out. If I can't be at your feet, then I cannot be. I live for each and every second with you and want to make you proud in everything I do.

Now I hope you understand why I: sleep on your clothes while you are away; have to be touching you when you are near (such as spooning with you, Mom, in our king-size bed or riding shotgun in your truck, Dad); wag my tail each and every time I see you; let my one-year-old brother Ethan share my food with me and never say a word; let my three-year-old brother Eddie lie on me like I am a blanket and never bat an eye; pose for a million pictures when Mom has the camera; lie on the kitchen rug in front of the stove while you are cooking with boiling water; give it my all during pheasant hunting; lie in the middle of your blueprints as you are diligently house planning; sit on top of puzzles as you are trying to finish them; sit in the bathroom with you when you are on the potty (even though my sense of smell trumps your sense of smell—this is true devotion!); enjoy car rides even when they are eight hours or longer down to see Grandpa and Grandma; try to walk up and down the steps on my good and bad days with you just so you can switch a load of laundry; follow you in and out of every room even when you are chasing Ethan to put a diaper on him; open the door with my head so I can be in the same room with you; lie on the rug in front of the sink when you are doing dishes; dream about you almost every time I am asleep; and look so frantically for anything to hold in my mouth to bring to you as a present when you come home.

You deserve everything, and I want to show you this. I wish I could give you more, such as a new wakeboard or an orange daylily, but I simply can't afford these lush items for you. Instead, I grab Mom's flip-flop or the nearest pillow and bring it to you like you are royalty because you *are* royalty to me. This is also the reason Mom has a hard time finding both of her flip-flops simultaneously.

Some people may think it is annoying with a big dog at their feet everywhere they go, but at your feet is where all dogs belong! Hopefully, my tale will get this message to dog owners across the world.

When I am sick and can't be at your feet, then it is time for me to go to Heaven. When I'm in Heaven, I can watch over you and protect you at any given moment like I have always done in the past. Please know that when I am no longer at your feet, my heart will always be wherever you are whether you are in a pheasant field, at a Jimmy Buffett concert, in a JC Penney portrait studio, or on our boat *Ruffin' It*.

Please do not be sad when I am gone. Instead rejoice for all of the amazing times that we experienced together. Dad, please remember me as the vivacious black puppy carrying firewood who chased you on your bike around the neighborhood. Mom, please remember me as the gentle doggie who would listen to you anytime you needed someone to listen. We have been through so much together.

I wish the entire world could experience the love I have experienced. It is amazing to me to watch "my people's" emotions for me day in and day out. I am only a dog, and as anyone can see, I am never treated like "just a dog." I watch as tears gently glide down Mom and Dad's faces while they are sitting with me on my weaker days. Tons of memories of our past adventures together fill their minds as their emotions keep pouring out. Sometimes, I am sorry to cause this much feeling. However, what purpose is life if we don't have these amazing connections with those we hold closest in our hearts?

Back to the Earth one day we will all go. Cherish the seconds with family and friends for now. Feel my presence and undying love every time the wind blows, you go fishing, or Mom gets the camera out. For that day when my "bow wow" is unable to be heard may be upon us sooner than we think. There is nothing I can do but be thankful for all of our days, each and every one of them.

You are getting more patient with me, Mom and Dad, because you know "my time" may be near. A few weeks ago, I had a small accident on the carpet. This was the first time that Mom did not get annoyed or upset. She finally said, "Gunther, this is the *least* I can do to help out and take care of you like you have done for us for many, many years." I admit, it is hard to accept help, but without help I can't make it these days. There are many people in this world who are aging and need similar help like I do. Be an advocate for yourself as much as possible, but say "please" and "thank you" when friends and family are there to help regardless of the situation. Please accept the help you deserve graciously as age takes its toll on you.

It is true when people get older that they stop caring about what everyone else thinks. Instead, they start doing the things they really have wanted to do all of their lives. Therefore, I say eat Milk-Bones constantly, snore as loud as you want, sleep upside down with your feet in the air, and cuddle as close as you can and as long as you can to anyone who means something to you. Life is uncertain and might not turn out as you hoped, so embrace each day and live. Mom and Dad, I don't know how long I can be here to trip you up in the kitchen and barge in behind you when you are trying to tuck the kids quietly into bed. As you can see, I will be at your feet as long as I am around.

I love you like a rock through anything and everything, and you have given light to all of my days. Thank you for letting me be at your feet for all of my years here. Please help me whenever you can. Although when you can't lift me anymore, let me be on my way and be free to guard you from above. As an angel, I can follow you every second of every day, and *believe me, I will!*

Please be at peace when my time has expired and know I have done my work here. God matched us up for a reason; I was meant for you and you were meant for me. We have coexisted for all of these years, and I need to know that you will be fine when my time has come. I will be on my way to adventures unknown that we all will experience in due time. I promise I will test the water for you first so you know what to expect.

Despite missing you terribly, I will be able to run, hunt, jump, and swim again in the big blue sky. I hope that you get more puppies in the future and create unique and fun memories with them. However, I pray when your time has come that I will be the first pooch you will look for in Heaven. You better believe I will be able to outrun any of your other dogs to feel you beside me again and hear you call my name. Just remember, I will wait for you forever and save you the best spot!

I sleep most of every day now because I feel constantly exhausted. I try my best to keep up with you every time you put laundry away, feed my "little brothers," take a shower, and do other daily activities. I feel extremely proud when you trip on me even though these times are very few as compared to our past together.

I also sleep a lot due to my inability to hear. As you know, I can't hear anything at all to help keep me awake or wake me up from my frequent naps. I wonder how Ethan's little voice sounds, and I question how it sounds when Eddie and Ethan are fighting because someone is not sharing. I wonder how it sounds when you say you love me because sadly I have forgotten this precious sound. For the longest time, I thought you were not talking to me for some crazy reason (of course, I thought this was really crazy for Mom because she talks all the time, even to herself).

Then I realized I couldn't hear anything, including the lawn mower, the stereo, the birds singing, and your cars coming home. Obviously, not hearing your voices is the most devastating part of losing my hearing. It sounds like a shell is constantly up to my ears, so I pretend that I am always hearing the crashing waves of Lake Michigan. This is a good but lonely sound. Thank God my vision is still good, so I can continue to read lips and protect you to the best of my ability. Our senses are crucial, and we take them for granted so often.

On a very sunny note, I can see that I woke up this morning to my sixteenth Christmas. God is good! Santa visited in the middle of the night. He left my "little brothers" a huge train table with the works and left Happy and me doggy treats in our festive paw-shaped stockings. In all these years, I still haven't caught Santa in the act or met any of his reindeer. Maybe I can meet them next year!

My one- and three-year-old "little brothers" were beyond excited this Christmas morning. The surprises for them just kept coming! It was so much fun to watch their eyes light up with excitement and their faces fill with joy. We got our pictures taken many times throughout the day. We enjoyed two yummy meals with our usual dog food plus juicy Christmas ham woven throughout. Surprisingly, I was able to get up and down rather easily and went outside multiple times to enjoy the beautiful cold snow on my paws and tummy.

As you can imagine, our house was an absolute mess after all of the presents were completely opened. This year I only opened one present because I slept through most of the festivities. Not a good showing compared to my past track record of opening presents but better than nothing.

We finished our day with singing "Happy Birthday" to Baby Jesus and even enjoyed Baby Jesus' birthday cake. Mom and Dad feel this is the most important part of the day, and I think it is the tastiest part of every twenty-fifth of December. Unfortunately, the day went way too quickly, and Eddie and Ethan were in bed before I knew it. Luckily, I was able to jump into bed by myself at the end of the day which I haven't done for months. Mom and Dad found me snuggled up in my king-size bed. They crawled in and cuddled next to me like many nights before that I've greatly missed.

Will I be here for next Christmas? I sure hope so, but we will see what is written in the stars for me. For now, hold my paws and hold me close. Let's cuddle, play, eat white cupcakes, live day to day, and savor each and every moment. Please enjoy me being at your feet because you know I will! I am going to put all of my other cares aside like eating all of the crumbs off the floor, picking up my toys, and checking every last inch of our yard's perimeter so I can enjoy what really matters in this world: wagging my tail when "my people" are with me, letting Eddie and Ethan give me goodnight hugs and kisses, smelling the fresh air, watching the sun glide down into the shimmering waters of Lake Michigan, playing trains with Eddie and Ethan, licking Happy's ears and letting her lick mine, cuddling with you, Mom, reminiscing with you, Dad, about all of our fabulous hunting stories, and *being at your feet*!

Acknowledgments

Thank you from the bottom of my heart to Gunther Denali for sharing your life with us and for your continuous inspiration, loyalty, and love; to my amazing husband Eric for sharing Gunther's journey and for your love and support every second of every day; to my wonderful parents for giving me a happy life and always believing in me regardless of what new adventures I begin; to my mother- and father-in-law for your constant optimistic outlook and playing with Eddie and Ethan frequently at Camp Love-a-Lot; to Eddie and Ethan for playing well together so Mommy could work on "Gunther's book" and for your "bigger than life" hugs that make me feel like I can accomplish anything; to Happy for your funny wiggles and frequent comic relief; to Debbie and Bill Jones for being my on-call editors and teaching me that grammar can be fun; to Stacey Bierling for editing, consulting, and creating a meaningful cover design; to Bill Stein for connecting *If I Can't Be At Your Feet* to the online world; to all of our friends and family for editing help and encouraging words throughout my writing journey; and to everyone who buys this book about an exceptional dog named Gunther Denali—may you also have a gold standard canine at some point in your lifetime. ☺